Brian Warner

19.1.85.

THE Genghis Khan GUIDE TO BUSINESS

Brian Warnes

8 HOLYROOD STREET
LONDON SE1 2EL
01-403 7575

1st Edition   Published March 1984
2nd Impression July 1984
3rd Impression October 1984

© OSMOSIS PUBLICATIONS

ISBN   0-9509432-0-7

Produced by Impart
Designed by Adrian Day
Printed in England by Howard Jones Printers Ltd.

ABOUT THE AUTHOR

Brian Warnes MA FCA, Fellow of the Royal Society of Arts, was educated at Wellington College Berkshire and St. Peters College Oxford where he obtained an Honours Degree in Natural Sciences (Physics). He is 47, married, with two children.

He held a temporary appointment at the Foreign Office where he handled a small £1m aid scheme for Nepal, his first direct experience of the inter-relationship between business and economic development.

"Wanting to find out more about business" he joined the London office of Peat, Marwick, Mitchell & Co. qualifying as a Chartered Accountant in 1964.

In 1966 he joined the Commonwealth Development Corporation, the British equivalent of the World Bank. He became part of a small team in Nairobi involved with tea and sugar plantations, housing developments, building societies, hotels (all originally start-ups), conventional industry and in particular CDC's "Devcos", development finance companies set up in each of the main capitals, Nairobi, Dar-es-Salaam, Kampala, specifically to finance small business.

Returning to England in 1972 he felt something similar was needed in the UK. He became part of the rescue team put into Spey Investments. Spey was a venture capital operation set up in the mid-60's with generous City and Pension Fund support, but which had not worked out as planned.

Hit by the 73/76 recession the Spey companies, as they were progressively restored to health, were quietly disposed of. Brian Warnes freelanced as a "company doctor" for a few months mainly to help complete the turn round of the Plastics Company mentioned in this book.

He was head-hunted into the National Enterprise Board where he was appointed a Deputy Divisional Director in charge of setting up a nation-wide small company funding operation.

Finding that such an operation needed the support that only a major clearing bank could give, he transferred to his present job in 1978. He is currently Managing Director of Midland Bank Venture Capital Limited which he set up in October 1979 as a new style, fast-acting, development and venture capital fund.

With its techniques now well bedded down (which closely follow the subject matter of this book) MBVC is already, in terms of number of companies, one of the fastest growing, larger equity funds operating in the UK market.

ACKNOWLEDGEMENTS TRIBUTES AND TESTIMONIALS

How this Book came to be written

At a meeting in January 1983 between the author and Eddie Ray, President of the Institute of Chartered Accountants in England and Wales, the idea was first mooted of setting down on paper the techniques that eventually became the subject matter of this book. The meeting was arranged on the kind introduction of Lord Benson, Adviser to the Governor of the Bank of England, and equally kindly, Ian Hay Davison, Senior Partner of Arthur Andersen & Co., Chartered Accountants.

After this auspicious start, a number of key people in industry have valuably helped mould the subsequent content by commenting on the relevant sections.

Tributes

Sir Kenneth Corfield, Chief Executive of Standard Telephones & Cables plc, which was until recently part of the giant American ITT group, of which he was also a director, and Chairman of The Engineering Council, is an engineer who started life as a small businessman making cameras. He comments (on an earlier draft) as follows:

> "It happens to express the self same principles that have contributed more to my own modest success than any other single factor of which I am aware.
>
> The importance of breakeven point and of testing the market value of a product or service by pricing it truly profitably seems so commonplace to us—and yet is so much neglected.
>
> The 'barrow-boy' mentality I may have practised but the phrase was first used in my presence by Mr. Hugh Barker, then Chairman of Parkinson Cowan Limited in the early sixties.
>
> Every year or so another company in my own province displays just the characteristics you so vividly describe. We have to change the management—perhaps your book will help more, otherwise intelligent, people to survive and help the Country.
>
> Every good wish for success."

At the other end of the scale, the production director of a small £¾m turnover company remarks:

> "I am bound to say I found it quite compelling reading, keeping me up until 2.30 a.m.—my wife thinks I'm mad!
>
> In general I think the style and presentation were marvellous. Not only did I understand it, I found I was actually enjoying reading it!
>
> Best wishes for its success."

To the author remarks such as these have been enormously heartening, in demonstrating that the "barrow-boy" understanding, on which all business rests, can indeed be quickly, accurately and successfully conveyed to the relative layman, given the right approach.

Appreciations

Thanks are also due to John Beevor, David Bloomfield, Robin Bellis-Jones, Brian Daubney, Paul Knill-Jones, Michael Franks, Sir Kenneth Sharp and the many others who have provided such invaluable comment on recurrent drafts; and in particular to Janet, my long suffering secretary, without whose good-natured, tolerant efforts on the word processor going well beyond the call of duty (often in the face of considerable aggravation) the book quite genuinely would never have appeared.

Finally, a word of very warm thanks to Grania and my family, to whom this book is dedicated, for all their kind help, sympathy and understanding while the midnight oil was being burned, night after night.

Author's View

It goes without saying that the views that follow are entirely the author's and do *not* necessarily represent the views of anyone mentioned above or in the book itself. Nor do they reflect the official or unofficial views of the Institute of Chartered Accountants or of the Bank or Fund for which the author works. Indeed, often the reverse. The book, to at least some extent, sets out to pioneer new ground . . . .

As will be evident from the discussion that follows, the book is priced in relation to the very considerable benefits it can bring to a company; and bring to all those associated with it, whether internally (shareholders, directors, employees), or externally (customers, suppliers, advisors, bankers, investors, and indeed the UK economy and employment in general).

INDEX

CHAPTER		PAGE
I	The Cliff-face Assignment	1
II	Magnificent Success, Magnificent Failure	11
III	The Breakeven Concept in Action	15
IV	Gross Margins	25
V	"Vulnerable" *v* "Safe" Businesses	33
VI	Cash Flow	39
VII	Stock and Debtor Requirement	45
VIII	Cash Flow Forecasting & Control	57
IX	Ensuring a Company is Adequately Financed	71
X	Business Plan–for a Service Company	83
XI	Dovetailing your Business to the Market	95
XII	Value Added	111
XIII	Sales Pricing	123
XIV	Production	133
XV	Improving Gross Margins	139
XVI	Company Doctoring	151
XVII	Control and Evaluation of Stock	155
XVIII	Conclusions	165
	Appendix–Detailed Cash Flow Formats	169

Chapter I

THE CLIFF-FACE ASSIGNMENT

Those who would like an immediate guide to business principles should turn to Chapter II. Chapter I provides some background.

Why the Genghis Khan Approach?
There are strong similarities between business and warfare. The market is a tough, fast-changing, rough-and-tumble, turbulent place. The Competition, particularly foreign competition, is ruthless and relentless. It will use every opportunity to damage you, to destroy you, to remove you from the scene altogether.

Equally you have to make the most strenuous effort to preserve, to protect, to care for your own side. The stronger you are the better you can protect. In modern terms the stronger the business sector, the more socially caring and compassionate a nation can be in looking after its own people.

In business as in warfare, therefore, you have to be very very determined and totally professional in order to win your objectives.

This book can do little about your determination.

It can, however, do much for your professionalism.

Is this a Definitive Guide?
Certainly. The critical "barrow-boy" factors that determine success, or failure, in business are relatively few in number and relatively straightforward in application.

The key issues are here gathered together, for the first time, all in one place in easily digestible form, for all who want to learn about them, or to learn more.

Who will benefit?
All those who want to know more about business—in every size of company, from the multi-national to the young marketing executive or engineer starting up in business for the first time, and the sole proprietor. Business principles are universal, whatever the size or detailed nature of the operation. Also all Accountants, Bankers, Consultants and all who provide training and educational services for business, like the Business Schools, Universities, Colleges of Further Education and Schools in general.

All who *think* they know about business: Businessmen, Bankers, Accountants, Consultants . . . . This Guide provides a Bench-Mark against which to assess your knowledge.

All types of business operation are covered by the techniques, manufacturing, service companies, contracting, distribution, retail, agriculture, and specialist operations like Charities and the Arts.

Down to Earth, Practical Guide

As the title suggests, this Guide makes few concessions. It is a tough, no holds barred, rigorously practical, day-to-day guide on running a business, stripped to its bare essentials.

Where the conventional wisdom gets in the way it has been ruthlessly discarded. Conversely where gaps appear in the conventional wisdom they have been made good with new techniques, as with the far-reaching subject of Breakeven (Chapter III onwards).

The methods were originally evolved in Spey, in the National Enterprise Board, in the Commonwealth Development Corporation for the really tough, "cliff-face" assignment, the rescue or start-up situation. Almost by accident they came to be applied to an established company in no particular difficulty. Immediately, management spotted ways in which performance could be improved: debt collection, profitability, cash flow. Other situations were looked at. The effects were in some cases dramatic. One company improved from a loss of £30,000 per month to a profit of £130,000 per month. Another moved from a loss of £1,000 per year to a profit of £5,000. A somewhat larger company moved from £1m pa loss to £1.7m profit. Sometimes it happened in months, sometimes over two to four years.

Business Perception, Business Understanding

Not all companies responded. Success appeared to depend, more than any other single factor, on the extent to which management could be given a perception of what *really* constitutes the nature of business, of how their own particular business worked, or could be made to work.

A significant feature began to emerge. Once the key elements were successfully being isolated, very special skills of interpretation and communication were neeeded to convey a real, pit-of-the-stomach, "gut-feel" for what was happening in the company to the management team, particularly to its non-financial members. It was done. How it was done and the precise formats used are set out in this book.

Strictly for the Layman

The issues are set out in strictly layman terms. They have to be strictly layman terms because the main beneficiaries, the sales team, the production team, the research and development team, as often as not the Managing

Director himself, the men and women on whom the whole operation is going to depend, are non-financial people. They have to understand, fully. No prior financial knowledge is thus needed. Indeed those that have it should perhaps set aside their existing knowledge for the time being whilst coming to grips with the possibly rather different concepts set out here.

The Barrow-Boy

There is the oft told story of a barrow-boy who drove a Rolls Royce, had a large house and went on holiday to the Caribbean every year. He was asked just why he was so successful. "It is quite simple", he said. "I buy for £1, sell for £2, and live very well on the 10% margin."

Business is more about buying and selling production hours, or "buying for £1 and selling for £2" (or £3 or £4), than about buying or selling products. Furthermore gross margin, not sales, constitutes the real income of a business. Companies whose management teams look at basic business issues in this way sharply improve their chances of success. Companies whose management teams ignore such issues—or, even more unhappily, do not seem to know about them—sharply diminish their chances of success.

Breakeven Point

Consider the question of breakeven point. A company that does not regularly measure its breakeven point—for the particular conditions of the moment—can greatly add to its difficulties of being able to operate successfully in its marketplace. This is particularly true during times of rapid change, during recessions, launching new products, opening new markets, taking advantage of sudden market opportunities. A convenient way of measuring breakeven point is given in the pages that follow. It greatly adds to the strength of any business operation, in good times or bad.

Importance of "Product Cash Flow" not "Product"

It is said, only half in jest, that the motto over the main entrance of a leading American company is "Our job isn't making steel, it's making money". The product is not, in itself, important. Its price/cost/demand relationship is. What follows should help you to identify, develop and use that relationship successfully for your own company.

The term "making money" does not mean making profits, so much as generating cash flow, although obviously the two are related. It is cash flow, not profit, that is the life-blood of a company. A company making a loss can sometimes have a stronger, more positive cash flow than one making a profit, absurd as it may seem (Chapter VIII).

In the last resort, unless the wages can be paid on Friday, every Friday, there will be no more Fridays on which to continue in business, however good the product potential and however good the skills of the management team. This book gives a number of examples of magnificent companies, with magnificent products that failed for one over-riding reason: *management did not sufficiently understand cash flow.*

Management Accounts

Very well run companies produce key "control" information weekly; it is on the Managing Director's desk by not later than midday the following Tuesday. If reports are produced less frequently than monthly or take appreciably longer than two to three weeks to appear, after the month's end, it is usually an indication of a "badly-run" company (with the occasional exception).

Again, management accounts based on the format of the traditional, year-end, Profit and Loss Account and Balance Sheet will contain only a relatively small part of the key information needed to run a company effectively. Paradoxically, such accounts also tend to be unduly long and complex and tend to be, therefore, unnecessarily time-consuming and confusing to producer and end-user alike. Something much briefer, something much more specific is needed.

Company Vulnerability

Companies that do not have sufficient management "bite" in these areas will appear unusually vulnerable to recessions, unusually vulnerable to competition, unusually vulnerable to the "Genghis Khan" approach of others.

On a national scale failure rates will be high. Those that survive will remain sluggish, get into undue trouble, lose out in their markets, fail to build-up strength quickly enough. Unemployment will be heavy; exports will be down; imports up; wage rates low. The economy itself will be "bumping along the bottom". Does this not have an all-too-familiar ring about it, when looking at the UK's economic performance over the years?

Foreign Expertise

Contrast the industrialists and businessmen in nearly all the other leading industrial nations, who *do* seem to know appreciably more about such issues: Gross Margin, Breakeven Point, Cash Flow, the real back of the envelope, nitty gritty of business. Such knowledge seems inseparable second nature, learnt from the earliest days of involvement with business; perhaps acquired even earlier during professional, school or university training. It may also be increasingly true of some of the newly-emerging industrial nations, in the Far East and elsewhere, who are now beginning to present such a formidable challenge to UK industry—almost certainly on account of this very factor.

Admirable Exceptions
There are of course magnificent exceptions, magnificent British companies who have done exceptionally well in national and international markets: GEC, Racal and others. Closer examination of these operations reveals the existence of those very features that account for business success in general, whether on the part of our foreign competitors or at home: a thorough-going knowledge of business and the sharpest possible instinct understanding and perception of it. Their very success illustrates what might be achievable if that same knowledge and understanding could only come to be applied throughout the UK scene.

Accountants and Bank Managers
Business needs the support of the professionals, Bank Managers, Accountants and Business Advisers in general. However, a structural problem seems to occur with certain aspects of their professional training, which is perhaps best illustrated by drawing on an analogy to highlight the vital distinction that needs to be made between "Statics" and "Dynamics".

"Statics" *v* "Dynamics"
There are two quite distinct aspects of your family car:
1) Its height, length, width, general shape, colour, size, style, comfort, interior layout and so on, all of which are **Static features**. They can be measured and evaluated when the car is **stationary**.
2) Its acceleration, road-holding, stopping power. These are **Dynamic features,** to do with the **motion** of the vehicle. They cannot be measured in any such way. **Indeed, how *do* you measure them?**

Business is no different. It of course needs its static measurements, like stock and debtor levels at the last Balance Sheet date; but it also needs the dynamic, to do with finding out where the company is *heading*. How rapidly is it gaining financial strength? Or losing it? Is the *rate* itself slowing down? Or accelerating? When will the cash run out? How does management, by conscious action, slow the process? Or stop it?

These are the questions that will be exercising the minds of the average management team on a day to day basis. They want to know what *next* year's balance sheet is going to look like, with as much advanced warning as possible, as much as last year's. If they do not like what they see, they want to know what to do about it, specifically. They want to know precisely what action to take to produce precisely what results.

Dynamics—a Different Scene
This cannot be done unless you know how to handle dynamic concepts. Unfortunately "Dynamics" forms an entirely separate branch of scientific measurement. (Indeed, originally, the problems were so acute in certain

areas of scientific measurement that a whole new branch of mathematics had to be invented to cope with the issues called differential calculus.) Those who have not been fully and specifically trained in the techniques will be helpless when confronted with problems that, in reality, are dynamic in nature, as with many of the underlying features of a growing, or declining, company.

It is certainly *not* the fault of the Accountants that they are ill-equipped to handle dynamic concepts, but of the training they receive. This needs to be put right quickly, but as can be appreciated it is not easy, with a whole new range of techniques required. A prime purpose of this book is to lay down the guidelines for others to follow.

Inevitably Accountants will benefit, in terms of job satisfaction, the importance of the role they play, enhanced self-esteem and valuable fee-earning work. So also will all those who take their financial knowledge from them including Bankers, Business Schools, and the majority of Businessmen.

The Excitment of Accounting

The Financial Times recently printed the following gem:

"Daddy, what's an Actuary?"

"An Actuary, my son, is someone who finds accounting too exciting".

It is an undeserved dig, at both professions, but this is the way many accountants, quite wrongly, feel about themselves. It is because they tend to deal in dry, historic, *static* figures from the *past*. Important though such figures are in the right context, businessmen also need Advisers who can stand shoulder to shoulder with them in *dynamically* pioneering a company into the *future*. It can be intensely exciting and rewarding work.

Hopefully, soon, this will be the radically changed image of the accountant:

Reprinted with kind permission of the Financial Times.

Noteworthy Exceptions
There are of course the most noteworthy exceptions. Some accountants, particularly those who have been able to learn "on the job" in industry for a number of years, are very effective indeed. The professions in general *do* support industry, closely, and are an invaluable part of the scene.

The Need to Upgrade Standards. The Need to Upgrade Professional Training
However, there is an inescapable feeling that training in the professions, good as it is, could be made very much better, in really coming to grips with the principles of business. At the moment too little of what appears in this book seems to be adequately covered in the formal training given to Accountants, Bankers or other professionals.

It might then even be possible to improve knowledge, inside and outside business, to the point of enabling UK companies actually to turn the tables on their foreign competitors and start making *them* worried about the inroads British companies are making into their markets . . . In theory, a company that has to ship its products from across the other side of the world, set up servicing, marketing and selling organisations 8,000 miles from home, *has* to be at a disadvantage compared to the local producer. There is no real reason why UK business should be suffering as much as it is from the tender attentions of the Japanese and others.

The Fundamental Role of the Engineer
It is evident, too, that the Engineer could and should be playing a much greater role in British business. He should be involved much more closely not only in the research and development, design and production functions but all the way up the management ladder to the Managing Directorship itself. It first requires a painstaking build-up of understanding, both on the part of the engineers themselves and within the companies to which their activities could be so valuable. This would then directly enable British companies to be more successful in meeting and beating foreign competition head-on.

Engineers *are* trained, very thoroughly, in the science of Dynamics. It is often an inseparable part of their job. A fundamental understanding of dynamics is needed for instance before an engineer can successfully design a "Guided" Missile: its "dynamic" features being of course that it can follow, hit and destroy its target, *even when the target takes deliberately evasive action.* There is a strong parallel between being able to target a missile to a certain performance and being able to target a company to a certain performance (cash flow, not profit), whatever the uncertainties of the environment in which it is operating.

Engineers wanting to learn more about business will subconsciously look for the dynamics of the situation. But, as explained, the financial world at the moment does not provide the dynamic picture needed, so there is nowhere for the engineers to start. Failing to pick up the threads correctly, they remain outsiders, much to the detriment of themselves and the British business scene. *Given the right training*, Engineers tend to make the best businessmen and to build up the strongest businesses, as the Japanese have found. In Japan 71,000 engineers qualify a year. In the UK, with about half the population, 6,000 engineers a year qualify; only a handful ever get into the centre of business (Chapter XV).

Why does a General Lack of Business Knowledge Seem to Exist in the U.K.?

The reason is probably cultural. Business for many years, since the mid 18th Century in fact, has quite falsely been downgraded as something "not quite nice". As a direct result, no book or training course adequately seems to cover the ground. The necessary business skills have not been evolved and codified into a form that can readily and easily be made available to all who need them.

"Feedback"

An overriding problem is also how to use the experiences of one company for the benefits of others. Those with wide knowledge of the inner workings of companies are struck by how often the same problems seem to recur, which could be avoided if only there was better knowledge of the experiences of others more widely available. Scientists overcome this "feedback" problem by analysing the results of their experiments and writing them up in detail, for the benefit of science and scientists at large, in, for instance, the monthly Physical Review.

The medical profession does likewise, publishing details of new drugs, new operations, new methods of treatment, in, for example, the British Medical Journal, in such a way as to avoid breaching patient confidentiality. Again this helps knowledge to spread quickly and accurately and avoids patients having to be used, effectively, as recurrent guinea pigs, with all the dangers, hardships and delays in arriving at foolproof methods of treatment that would otherwise be involved. Particularly important, of course, is the need for rapid communication on drugs and treatments that do *not* work and are actively harmful.

Case Histories

In contrast, the UK business scene has no such source of regular case-history information available to it in quite the same way. Provided adequate steps are taken not to harm any current commercial operation, by taking examples from a former period or under a different management, real-life case histories *can* be used to illustrate vital business issues, as indeed is attempted here. Furthermore by highlighting the experiences of larger companies, with all their resources, the exercise demonstrates how very careful the relatively small company has to be to get its techniques right. A special word of thanks is thus due to all the named and unnamed companies whose case histories so vividly illustrate, reinforce and highlight the main themes of this book.

Role of Improved Business Understanding in Reducing Unemployment

Given this knowledge and perception right across the board, unemployment in the UK should be significantly reduceable, if not "at a stroke" then certainly within a timescale measurable in months and years rather than decades. If only 10% of the 110,000 businesses that fail every year could be saved through better business perception, 50,000 to 100,000 jobs a year might be saved. The effect would be cumulative.

It is not only the young and frail businesses that would benefit. There are one million businesses in the UK with turnovers of up to £100,000 pa; another two hundred and seventy five thousand with turnovers of between £100,000 and £500,000; and another ninety two thousand over £500,000. If only 10% or 20% of all these companies could become stronger, more durable, trade more successfully, take on more staff, invest more, export more, replace more imports, perhaps even several hundred thousand new jobs could be created; again with cumulative effect.

50,000 companies suddenly becoming more confident of the business issues and taking on, say, 20 more people each would lift one million off the unemployment register. When the techniques of this book were introduced to one small company, it increased employment from 38 to 54 and a subcontractor from 19 to 30 in just four months. So it *can* be done.

Conclusion

If what follows succeeds in its aim, by the time you have read it and absorbed the full gut-feel for the issues it is trying to portray, you will *know* just what you must do to get the right answers in business.

You will then start applying those same lessons to your own company and getting a considerable kick, thrill and excitement out of doing so. You won't necessarily succeed. Your product or service may, at the end of the day, simply not be good enough. But it won't be for lack of trying.

Conversely, if you do begin to win through, your success will by that much more certain, the stability of your company that much more durable, the rewards that much more satisfying.

These, then, are the challenges issued to all who read this book. Good luck.

Chapter II

MAGNIFICENT SUCCESS MAGNIFICENT FAILURE

The * * * * Bank Manager

You are the Managing Director of your Company, or the Sales Director, or the Production Director, or the Finance Director; or a Banker, Accountant Engineer, Consultant or Academic associated with it. You have a good product, or you think you have, and it sells, or is about to sell, reasonably well. You have either just started in business or have been operating for some, or many, years. You think you have enough funding for your company, but at the crucial moment your Bank Manager suddenly gets a bit restive and you have to divert time and energy to get him to go on supporting you, or to provide more.

But perhaps, having helped you on two or three occasions already with increased facilities, he is becoming more and more difficult to convince. You have that big order just around the corner, or maybe have already landed it, but he seems remarkably reluctant to provide the extra working capital you are obviously going to need.

Maybe your order book is an all time record and your customers are pushing for delivery, but despite all your best efforts you just don't seem to be able to get work out of the door. Cash is fast running out and again the Manager is unsympathetic.

Perhaps, conversely, you are in actual trouble. You have increased the sales force, intensified advertising and cut prices to stimulate volume, but losses seem to be mounting, even if sales do begin to forge ahead.

Alternatively, markets may be actively falling away. Sales and order intake levels may be actually down, despite all your efforts. Again, cash is beginning to run out. The bank is even beginning to make noises about *reducing* the facility.

Survival

Whichever of these scenarios faces you, this book is designed to help; to help you, at the most basic level, to survive, more or less regardless of the economic climate.

Success

Survival is one thing. Whatever the starting point, you want to succeed. A company making just £8,000 per month can be worth anything up to £1m on the Unlisted Securities Market. In exceptional cases, one making £0.5m could be worth £10m. Continental Microwave, set up in 1979, was launched on the USM in May 1982 with profits of £175,000 and priced at 260p a share. Just seven months later the shares were already changing hands at 800p, valuing the Company at £3.5m.

Racal, set up in the 50's, has been a particularly outstanding success. Why, in contrast, was Rolls Royce, at least immediately prior to 1971, such an outstanding failure? Why did a good company like Kenwood nearly fail in its formative years? It had a magnificent product, a world beater, or at least a very good food beater. Why did The British Motor Corporation, with superb engineering skills, as embodied in the Mini, get into such trouble? Why in contrast is GEC, which supports some of the toughest industries in the book like electrical transformers, piling up a cash mountain that if it were food instead of money, with an 'E' in its name instead of a 'G', would be the subject of national and international wonder at the sheer productive scale of the operation?

Failure

How did a company with products and technical ingenuity as brilliant as Ferranti's get into sufficient trouble to need rescue by the NEB? Likewise, ICL or Cambridge Instruments or Sir Clive Sinclair? All, thankfully, have survived to fight another day and have subsequently become magnificent commercial operations. But what if the necessary rescue effort had not been available when needed? What of the myriad of other potentially fine companies that, for one reason or another, were not rescued, or not rescued in time, over the past few decades? Their loss has been a national tragedy. How can the same be avoided in future? Hopefully this book, by highlighting some of the more obvious pitfalls, will play its part in helping you to understand what went wrong and how to avoid the same happening to you.

The Barrow-Boy

Why in contrast to these magnificent failures does your local barrow-boy, selling some very ordinary products off a very ordinary barrow, seem able to manage that odd holiday in the Caribbean every year?

"What do you expect?" the cynic will say. "Wink, wink, nudge, nudge, the archetypal cash business," implying that at least some of the takings never see the light of the taxman's day.

But on examination the real reason is rather different. The concentration on cash is indeed pre-eminent. If anyone understands business it is the barrow-boy. He is a market trader par-excellence. At any moment of the day he knows exactly what he can, what he must, get for his product and this may change several times a day. It may change on Tuesday compared with Monday. It may change between the second week of December and the third week in January. Above all cash is paramount, the need to keep it turning over, the need to keep it earning its keep. *That* is why he is so successful.

Business "Understanding", Business "Perception"

The barrow-boy writes little down, but he carries in his mind's eye an exact understanding and perception of his business, from day to day, from hour to hour, from minute to minute. The really successful businessman, however big his company, will have that same perception, that same understanding, in his mind's eye. It will be an inseparable part of his every thought, an inseparable part of his every action. He will ensure the management information he uses dovetails very precisely with that perception, which will rigorously dictate its form, content and timing.

Speed of Information

The key information a barrow-boy needs, if written down, could be written on the back of an envelope. It has to be brief, because he needs it very, very quickly to guide his every move. However large a business, approximate accuracy and speed is always preferable to full precision produced weeks after the event. Given sufficient ingenuity, profitability can even be measured daily, as it happens, from invoices of goods leaving the despatch department for instance. You can always check how accurate such rule of thumb, back of the envelope, techniques are by seeing if the month-end accounts faithfully reflect the initial view they give and, if they do not, by progressively improving them until they do.

Conclusion

It is the purpose of this book to try and give you that heightened perception, to give you that increased gut-feel, however much, or little, knowledge you start with. The result, hopefully, will be self-evident in the performance, the durability, the success of your company. Above all, properly grasped, the exercise should be, quite simply, enormous FUN.

Chapter III

THE BREAKEVEN CONCEPT IN ACTION

Bench-Mark

Measurement has little meaning unless there is a bench-mark against which to relate it. The maps a surveyor produces would be of little use without the concept of Mean Sea Level for instance.

There is perhaps no more fundamental dividing line in business than between whether a company is making a profit or whether it is making a loss. It is as fundamental as the dividing line between Sea and Land. So let's introduce the concept of **Breakeven Point**, the level of sales you need just to cover all costs.

Once a company's operation settles down, its breakeven point should begin to stabilise at a more or less pre-determined figure. If this figure can be accurately measured and carried in the mind's eye of all the members of the management team as they run the company on a day-to-day basis, they will know at once whether it is profitable or not, and to what extent.

Breakeven Versus Sales and Orders

If a company breaks even at £22,000 turnover per month, £1,000 per working day, it is self evident that it must be profitable if it is dispatching more than £1,000 worth of goods a day, and lossmaking if less. In the first instance, that is the *only* relationship management need monitor.

It is equally possible to look forward and see what is going to happen in the future from the order-intake level. If weekly order intake is running at an average of less than £1,000 per day, and stays below that level despite all the efforts of management to get it up, the company is clearly in trouble. Comparison of order intake against breakeven point is therefore an invaluable early warning system.

Trends

Furthermore, if the company is operating at above breakeven, is the gap between sales and breakeven getting bigger, and therefore are profits getting better? Or smaller and getting worse? And if so, at what rate? If it is operating below breakeven, is the gap getting smaller and the lossmaking therefore reducing? This immediately gives a vision of the future, of when the company should come into profit and of how long it will take.

"Wait a minute", you will be saying "what is the difference between measuring the monthly build-up of sales and orders, which all companies do as a matter of course, and measuring the movement in the *gap* between such figures and breakeven?"

It is here where the "dynamic" concept, correctly applied, can open up whole new worlds for a company. If a company is lossmaking and the management team is focussing just on sales and order intake, it is natural to think the *only* way to reduce losses is to increase sales.

Two Possibilities for Action

However, if management focus instead on **the Gap between Breakeven and Sales,** *two* possibilities open up:

(1) to try and increase sales, as before, but now even more powerfully,
(2) to get breakeven point down.

In the latter case all that matters is that breakeven point should successfully be brought *down to under sales,* whether or not sales themselves move ahead as hoped.

Something still more startling follows. If it is the *Gap* between sales and breakeven that matters, *provided a lossmaking gap is successfully closed, it cannot matter at what sales volume this happens. It could just as well happen at one-half or even one-quarter of present sales volumes, as at increased volumes.*

Therefore even if measures to reduce breakeven point have the unpalatable consequence of also reducing sales, it cannot matter provided the rate at which breakeven falls outpaces the rate of fall-off in sales.

Measuring Breakeven

Let's now look at a rule of thumb method for measuring where actual breakeven point lies. First a digression is necessary on the meaning of Gross Margin.

Fixed and Variable Costs

These are two fundamentally different types of cost in a company; those that happen anyway, which are a product of time, like salaries, rates, vehicle running, office costs, etc.; and those that *only* happen if product is being manufactured and sold, like material costs, delivery costs, etc.

The first type of cost is known as **Fixed Cost** or **Overhead Cost**. Appropriately enough it is known in America as "period" cost, reflecting the "time" element (which, it should be mentioned, has nothing to do with "historic" cost).

Variable Costs

The second type of cost is known as **Variable Cost** or **Direct Cost**, because it varies in direct proportion to physical activity in the business. For those in any doubt about the concept, a better term might be **"Product" Cost**. The concept sometimes gives rise to argument about whether such-and-such a cost does indeed vary with productive output and therefore whether it properly constitutes a genuine variable cost. Labour is the prime example. Direct production workers cannot be hired and fired (thankfully) with every small change in output. Labour cost is therefore, in reality, more in the nature of a fixed cost so the argument goes.

Later in this book, full precision will be achieved by introducing the concept of value added per hour where labour is treated as neither a fixed nor a variable cost, which further simplifies the task of explaining the basic issues and provides the fully accurate approach. For the moment, labour cost will be treated as a variable cost, which is sufficiently exact for present purposes.

Summary

All costs can therefore be divided into those that exist and accrue with time, regardless of the amout of physical product or (service) activity taking place within the company—the "fixed costs"; and those only incurred because of such activity—the "direct", "variable" or "product" costs.

Gross Margin

It is the latter costs that mainly concern us here. The dynamic behind the concept, costs that physically "move" and increase or decrease in direct relation to activity, is the dynamic that lies behind the most fundamental of all concepts in business, the concept of gross margin.

Gross margin is the gap between sales and variable costs. It is the margin that is left after deducting the variable costs from sales. It constitutes the *real income* of the business.

If £40 of direct material cost, £20 of labour cost and £5 of delivery cost are incurred in producing every £100 of goods sold, the real income of the business is £35.

Gross Margin Percentage

The £35 is known as the **Gross Margin** of the company. It can be expressed as a percentage of sales, 35% in this case, to give the **Gross Margin Percentage**. 35% gross margin percentage expresses the dynamic that whatever the sales level of the business, real income will be only 35% of it.

Real Income

Note the word "only". Real income of a business may only be a fraction of apparent (sales) income. Managements who overlook, or are not fully aware of this concept, can soon find their companies in serious trouble and be at a loss to know what to do about it.

Some Examples

Here are some examples for you to work through for yourself.
What is the real income of the following businesses:

Figure 1

Sales £	GM %	Gross Margin £
1000	10%	?
250	40%	?
333	30%	?
500	20%	?
800	12·5%	?

The answer of course is £100 in each case.

Now we come to an absolutely critical next step. Turn the calculation round and find out what level of sales is needed, at the gross margin percentages shown, to produce £100 of gross margin (the answers are given on page 33):

Figure 2

Gross Margin £	GM %	Sales £
100	5%	?
100	10%	?
100	20%	?
100	25%	?
100	30%	?
100	40%	?
100	50%	?

It will be seen that the first column divided by the second gives the answer:

100   divided by   0·05   equals   2000   etc.

£100 of gross margin means real income of £100. Suppose now that the total fixed overhead cost of the business is also just £100. Real income will then exactly equal fixed cost, will exactly "cover" it, at all the sales levels shown—a fact which you might like to ponder on . . .

Breakeven Point

The first column can be retitled "Total Fixed Costs". What has been calculated in the third column *is the level of sales needed just to breakeven*, or the Breakeven Point at the fixed overhead level of £100. The third column can be retitled accordingly.

We thus come to *the* most fundamental and most important relationship in business.

Figure 3

$$\frac{\text{FIXED COST}}{\text{GROSS MARGIN PERCENTAGE}} = \text{BREAKEVEN POINT}$$

Uses

What can we do with it?

The significance of say a 30% gross margin percentage is that every £100 of sales produces £30 of real income.

Below breakeven point, the whole of this gross margin will contribute towards reimbursing fixed costs; not all fixed costs, only a proportion of them—because the company is operating below breakeven.

Quantifying Loss

Suppose a company has a £10,000 breakeven point at 30% gross margin. A sales level of £7,000 would then contribute towards, or reimburse, 7/10ths of total fixed costs as follows:

Figure 4

	£			£		
Sales	7,000	@ 30%	=	2,100		
Less: Breakeven	10,000	@ 30%	=	3,000	=	Fixed Costs
Shortfall	(3,000)			(900)		

A loss of £900 thus results from the shortfall in sales of £3,000 which of course may be found directly by taking 30% of £3,000.

Quantifying Profit

Conversely if sales of £15,000 are achieved:

Figure 5

	£			£		
Sales	15,000	@ 30%	=	4,500		
Less: Breakeven	10,000	@ 30%	=	3,000	=	Fixed Costs
Excess above Breakeven	5,000			1,500		

£1,500 profit is made, on sales £5,000 above breakeven (30% of £5,000).

"Quick" Profit/Loss

Given that, in a well-run company, monthly breakeven point and gross margin percentage should stabilize at broadly the same level each month (depending however on sales mix as discussed more fully from Chapter XI onwards) management need only know the monthly sales figure to determine monthly profitability. (Similarly for weekly, or daily, profitability.) Furthermore, from the order intake for the month it is possible to gain some idea of where future productivity will lie (once the work has been planned into the months in which it is going to be delivered).

The Implications

A veritable cornucopia of techniques then opens up to help companies to survive in virtually any type of market, good or bad, by deliberately "moving" their breakeven point.

It is a statement of the obvious, of course, but the point needs making. Events in the outside world, your markets and your level of sales, are not within your control. Events within the company, your breakeven point, *are* largely within your control.

Forcing Breakeven Point Down

Supposing in the above loss-making example, where sales of £7,000 were achieved at a breakeven level of £10,000, you decided to force down your breakeven point to under £7,000. This would be a more immediate course of action than trying to get sales up past £10,000. (You want to make a profit, of course, so need to get *above* breakeven.)

Breakeven point can self-evidently be reduced by:

(1) Cutting fixed costs;
(2) Improving gross margin percentage.

Let's cut £600 off fixed cost, taking it back to £2,400, and improve margins to 40%. Breakeven point is then what? You might like to work it out for yourself. You will find the company now makes £400 profit at existing sales levels and will achieve breakeven if it loses, say, £1,000 worth of sales as a result of hardening gross margins. Consider the implications in strategic terms.

Size of Market

Suppose your company breaks even at sales of £100,000 per *month*. You are clearly in trouble if the size of your market, which you will not have to yourself but will be sharing with others, totals only £1m per *annum*.

On the other hand, if just two of you share a £10m market, you should be very content.

Again, if you have enjoyed a £10m market and it suddenly drops to £5m, you are clearly in trouble unless you react very quickly.

Reacting to Market Drop

How do you react? You react by reducing your breakeven point, however painful and traumatic. What you do *not* do is hope the market lull is only temporary and soldier on hoping for better days. Such an attitude has been the graveyard of countless thousands of British companies, wiped out by each new recession that hits. The loss of these, often very fine, companies has been irretrievable. There is no need for *you* to follow their example, even in quite difficult markets.

Recessions perfectly Normal

Recessions follow one another with the constancy and inevitability of waves in a sea. They are a perfectly normal, regularly recurring, part of the business scene, not an aberration or an exception. So the well-found business has to learn to cope with them and, indeed, profit from them.

Have you ever heard of a barrow boy complaining about recession? He makes his "turn" whether the market is going up, or going down. He has the capacity to scale *back* his business just as often and just as effectively as to expand it forward.

Going Forwards

Often companies seem only to know how to go forwards. They react to falling turnover by cutting prices, by increasing costs and by trying to sell more, which as often as not merely hastens and precipitates the very end they are so strenuously trying to avoid. Armageddon.

Scaling Back

Those who succeed use equally forceful techniques for moving backwards, knowing how to close a loss-making gap by selling less rather than selling more. Properly used, this approach can considerably enhance a company's real strength, good market conditions or bad.

Surviving Recessions

A company that has this capacity will find it can emerge from recessions financially stronger and better placed than might otherwise be the case. If it achieves this more successfully than its competitors, by suffering less than they do, it should be able to gain market opportunity and gain market share. In such circumstances recessions are almost to be welcomed!

This is just what fit, foreign companies have been doing in the UK scene over the past 20 or 30 years. By maintaining their strength, in good times and bad, they have been able to rampage widely over the field.

Reacting to Increased Sales

Having got your breakeven point right in relation to your market, what you should *not* do is to allow it to rise with rising sales; or at least not allow it to rise more than you have to. You want to take the benefit of those extra sales into your Profit and Loss Account and Cash Flow, not throw it away.

So accurate monitoring of your breakeven point is crucial. What was it last week? What is it this week? What will it be next week?

For once you know, you have an immediate insight into your profitability, down to the last invoice. You can begin to "trade" in the market place, just as the barrow boy "trades".

The "Price"/"Volume" Relationship

Suppose a stall costs £40 per day to run. Once sufficient product has been sold to cover the "overhead" of £40, prices can be sharply altered. They can be altered *downwards* if more is earned by selling the rest in quantity at low prices than by holding prices and selling less. They can be altered *upwards* if there is more to be gained by selling less at higher prices, even if goods are left on the stall at the end of the day. There is clearly a relationship between price and volume, which needs to be very precisely identified if the right decisions are to be made.

The skill—and fun—in running your company lies, of course, in measuring that relationship, which may vary from day to day, product to product, market to market and season to season, so your measuring processes need to be equally prompt and flexible. You can then design your whole operation to maximise the benefits and minimise the pitfalls.

"Market-Led" v "Product-Led"

This brings us to a key point, which will recur in what follows. You, of course, stand to gain more if you successfully identify the natural characteristics of your marketplace and fit your product range and method of operation into those characteristics, than if you simply come up with a product for a product's sake, a better widget, and try to force it onto an unsuspecting market-place.

Our overseas competitors are particularly good at this approach. The product concept, styling, service, reliability, etc. is market-led. It starts with the market and ends with the product, not the other way round. The operation is then structured to produce viability, that is to say to achieve a low breakeven point in relation to market potential. That is why the foreign competitors appear so successful, in contrast to the many British companies who so often seem so unwarrantably damaged by their efforts. Viability has to be built into the product at the design stage, in the light of reality about market need, a theme developed more fully from Chapter XI onwards.

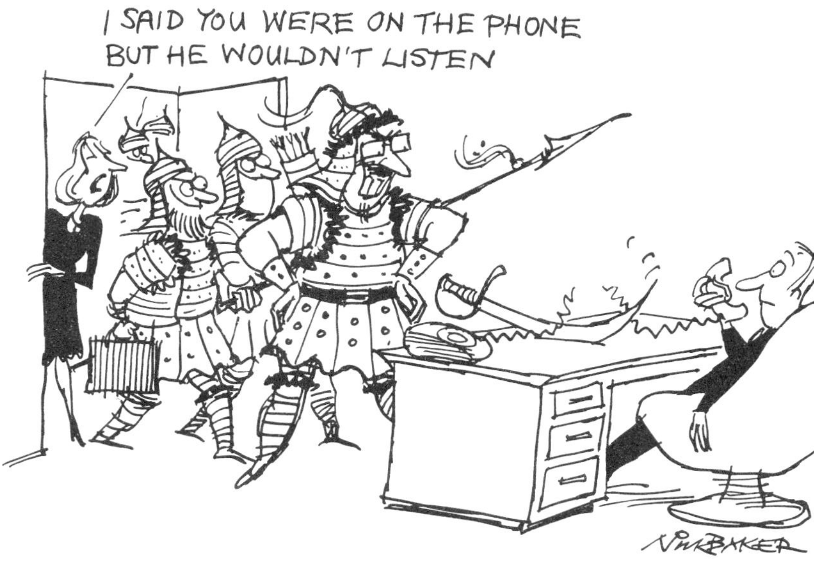
I SAID YOU WERE ON THE PHONE
BUT HE WOULDN'T LISTEN
NICK BAKER

Chapter IV

GROSS MARGINS

Achieving Good Margins

The greatest scope for reducing breakeven point lies in improving gross margins. It is not, of course, easy, otherwise everybody would be doing it. If you simply put up prices above the competitive level, you will quickly be left with no business. Some guidelines on the alternatives will follow later, but the point illustrates the view that margins are an indicator of management toughness and of the extent of management's business understanding.

Increasing Prices, deliberately allowing Volume to fall

Initially let us concentrate on the price aspect. Of course the lower the existing gross margins are the smaller the price rises needed to achieve quite disproportionate improvements.

Ignoring, for the sake of simplicity, a slight imprecision in the arithmetic (see caveat on page 27) a 10% price increase in a product presently achieving 10% gross margin doubles the margin in money terms, i.e. doubles real income.

The not at all evident conclusion is that such a company needs to sell only *half* as much volume as before to achieve the same real income.

So if the 10% price rise causes a drop in volume there is little need to worry, if it does not cause the company to lose more, in this case, than half its business! So you can put up prices, quite content to see volume fall back radically.

How Far can Sales Volume be allowed to fall?

We have just seen how a company operating at, say, 10% gross margin will double its real unit income by putting up prices by a mere 10%:

If the higher prices depress sales volume by less than 50%, the company is better off in real terms. And it is incomparably better off if sales volumes drop considerably less, say by only 10%:

Figure 6

EFFECT OF 10% SALES PRICE INCREASE

	Before £	After £
Unit Sales Price	100	110
Unit Cost of Sales	90	90
Unit Gross Margin	10	20

Figure 6a

	Before	After
No. of Units Sold	1,000	900
Gross Margin	£10,000	£18,000

Real income increases by a formidable 80%.

What happens when Prices are *cut* to *increase* Sales Volume?

If a company operating at 20% gross margin cuts its prices by, say, a mere 10% to stimulate volume, it is incomparably worse off until volume has more than *doubled!*

If, for instance, the 10% cut in sales price stimulates only 10% increase in sales volume, this is what happens:

Figure 7

EFFECT OF 10% SALES PRICE CUT

	Before	After
Unit Sales Price	100	90
Unit Cost of Sales	80	80
Unit Gross Margin	20	10
No. of Units Sold	900	990
Gross Margin	£18,000	£9,900

Real income is nearly *halved*.

The Nature of the Misconception
Gross Margin not Sales constitutes the Real Income of a Business.

Those not aware of this fundamental rule can easily be forgiven the "common sense" approach of trying to get out of a loss-making situation by attempting to *increase* sales. The easiest way to improve sales quickly is to cut prices and to intensify advertising, marketing and other costs. *Fixed costs* are thus *increased;* and *gross margins* are simultaneously *reduced. Both factors combine to push up breakeven point, often by far more than the increase in sales achieved. The gap between sales and breakeven widens, perhaps dramatically* (Figure 3).

Caveat

Note that in figure 7 gross margin reduces from 20% to 11% (10/90) *not down to exactly half*. A doubling or halving of gross margin *in money terms* does *not* mean a doubling or halving in *percentage terms*. Care is thus needed in the choice of terms.

Case Histories

When, in 1958, The British Motor Corporation brought out the record-breaking Mini, it was priced at the level to be "competitive" with the Ford Popular. The sales side would also have had in mind the need to fix prices at a level low enough to keep the very expensive "volume" production lines full. Obviously the lower the sales price was kept, the more likely this was to happen.

Breakeven *v* Production Capacity

BMC, like, for instance, Rolls Royce, was run by some very fine engineers. They were operating in an environment, however, where the brute-force, barrow-boy concepts of the kind set out in this book seem not to have been widely known about on the UK scene. (This is still true, incidentally, in many UK companies, but not, of course, in BL since the advent of the new management approach in 1977.)

As explained later, management accounts are the mirror-image of management's own perception of business. Graham Turner, in his book "Business in Britain" published in 1969, speaks on page 381 of a "major weakness" of BMC being "insufficient management information" and goes on to say "John Barber, BL's Director of Finance and Planning thinks it was so serious it would have been difficult to know anything was wrong until it stuck out like a sore thumb".

It thus seems unlikely that the engineers and marketing men running BMC in the 50s and 60s would have had sufficient key monthly management information at their side to guide them. If so, they would not have been able to make sufficient distinction between fixed and variable costs, or accurately measure gross margins, or adequately measure where breakeven point in fact lay.

It is impossible to reconstruct exactly what happened in BMC all those years ago but one guess is that the effects of "over-engineering" the Mini, resulting in high labour and material costs coupled with setting low sales prices, meant the Mini production line may have had to work day in and day out, week in and week out, year in and year out, at over 93% capacity just to breakeven. (Some claim breakeven point was in fact well over 100%, for at least periods during the 60s and 70s.)

Without the breakeven concept, or sufficient underlying management information on which to base it, management would not have been alerted to the rack onto which they were placing the company. In most production lines consistently maintaining 70% production capacity is hard enough, given holidays, down time, strikes etc., let alone 93%.

Dauntingly, this also, of course, left a mere 7% above breakeven to achieve profitable sales!

Crunch

Clearly the company was on a hiding to nothing. As long as this policy lasted it *had* to fail, from the moment the first Mini rolled off the production line. The average price of a Mini moved from £497 in 1959 to only £739 by 72/73 a full 14 years later. The operation that became BLMC in 1968 did fail, but many years, tens of thousands of jobs and hundreds of millions of pounds later.

The Opening given to Overseas Importers

Apart from the tragedy in terms of jobs alone, what an opening it gave for foreign importers who did get their sums right. It also resulted in permanent damage, not just to BMC, but to whole sections of British industry. Raw material suppliers like British Steel and a whole raft of component suppliers and sub-contractors suffered severely, if not fatally. The long-suffering tax-payer had to support a multi-billion pound rescue operation, happily with a management team since 1977 who *do* understand the issues.

Scope for Raising Prices

At one stage the Mini was priced at around £500, was highly thought of, selling well, and was cheaper than any seriously competing product. It is doubtful whether an extra £100 to £150 added to the price would have had any great effect on its selling ability. Guessing that at £500 the Mini was generating around £100 to £150 (20% to 30%) gross margin an increase in price to £600 to £650 would have doubled gross margin in money terms. As in so many companies, a relatively small percentage change in price would have had a much larger effect on gross margin, real income.

Effect in Forcing Down Breakeven Point

This would also have had the effect of sharply reducing breakeven point. In companies where labour can be treated as a genuine variable cost, a doubling of gross margin in money terms halves breakeven point. In capital-intensive businesses like car production lines, labour is more of a fixed cost and the reduction is not quite so dramatic, but it is still substantial.

The extra £100 to £150 earned per car would, at a guess, have reduced breakeven point from 93% of production capacity down to around 60% to 70%, the proper target area. At 60% to 70% capacity:

(1) A line is much more comfortable to run, consistently. In particular strikes cannot damage a company to anything like the same extent.

(2) In addition much greater scope is given for producing good profits once the company gets into the, now much larger, 30% area above breakeven.

The "Self-Generated" Cash Flow higher pricing would have achieved

Between 1959 and 1977 Leyland sold over 4¼ million Minis. If each one had been priced just £150 higher, and assuming no loss of volume, Leyland by 1977 would have been better off to the extent of up to £637 million. (£1·5bn, if the benefit of having the cash available for reinvestment is taken into account.) Allowing for the gross margin and variable cost element, 10% loss of volume resulting from these higher prices could still have produced up to an extra £507m, 20% loss up to £378m, 30% up to £248m, and so on. For just this one model.

The money could have been ploughed back into R & D, marketing, new design, on the scale that has taken place in the foreign competitors who are now providing such formidable competition to the UK car producers. What marvellous new designs could have followed the Mini, enabling them in turn to dominate their markets . . . .

Many business operations in the 50s and 60s were governed by the economies of scale syndrome. The larger the scale of the operation, so the argument went, the lower the unit cost. Larger and larger groupings were forged, like BLMC in 1968, and more and more sophisticated mass production lines were set up.

This was fine, so long as the market existed to keep them full. Suppose a production line costing £5m p.a. to run produces 10,000 units at full capacity. Theoretical cost would be £500 per unit at full capacity, £1,000 at half capacity (if the distinction between fixed and variable costs was not sufficiently appreciated), £2,000 at one quarter capacity and so on. Common sense dictated that the fuller the line could be kept, the lower the price that needed to be imposed in the market place.

This was then turned round into the argument "we must keep sales prices down to whatever level is appropriate to keep the lines full", usually going further than was necessary to make sure. Here all the trouble began because it was insufficiently realised that more could be lost in reduced prices than gained in reduced costs. The benefit side was not looked at in relation to the cost. This also made companies peculiarly vulnerable to recessions. Prices were slashed in often fruitless attempts to keep works full. Single-minded preoccupation with "volume" all too easily blinded management to all other considerations.

A Happier Case History

An almost identical example was encountered in 1973 where management *was* alerted to the problem in time. As a direct consequence it *was* put right.

The company, set up a few years before, was the UK subsidiary of a large, successful US corporation with sales of over $250m per year.

It was a fairly big plant with four thermoforming lines capable of producing up to 2m units a day. Not unnaturally, competition from established UK companies, who wanted to keep the newcomer out, was intense. So prices had to be cut to get volume up quickly. It *was* steadily building up, 30% of capacity, 40%, 50%. . . .

Losses were heavy, but losses were expected with a "volume" plant until, on the US pattern, around 70% capacity was reached. Thereafter substantial profits were projected.

Oil prices suddenly quadrupled as the 1973/74 recession hit. Prices had to be pared even finer in near desperate attempts to maintain volume. Sales efforts were intensified, inevitably involving sharp cost increases. But the very "success" of these policies, in stimulating further volume, resulted in losses increasing, rather than, as expected, decreasing.

Breakeven Measurement

No calculation had been made of where the breakeven point did in fact lie, particularly in relation to the conditions of the time. When it was measured, far from coming out at around 70% of capacity, it came out at just over 140%! Quite apart from the evident absurdity of having to operate at better than that level to get into profit, that rate of output, in the conditions of the time, represented nearly twice attainable market size, the market itself having shrunk in the recession.

Breakeven Point Forced Down

The Board meeting that followed lasted for the best part of twelve hours. First and foremost, despite the apparent impossibility of winning higher prices from a severely competitive and stretched market-place, breakeven point *had* to be brought down to a sensible level of around 70% and if possible lower.

Over the next two or three years it was done, using many of the techniques set out in this book and today the company is a thriving, secure, durable, and confident operation employing many hundreds of people. None of the key management team, Managing Director, Sales Director, Production Director, Finance Director nor any of their senior staffs changed. The improvement was brought about by a first class management team acquiring a slightly altered, but crucially different, business approach and perception.

Management "Perception", Management "Understanding"

One of the more memorable moments during the marathon Board meeting was when the Sales Director stood up and said:

"Mr. President, amidst all this gloom and despondency"—the Sales Director was British—"there is at least one bright ray of sunshine. Mr. Snooks, my most senior Sales Manager, last year single-handedly sold over £1m of product, the first time anyone has achieved that in the company's history. I think he should be congratulated".

He was considerably nettled by the reply:

"He should be sacked. With discretion to fix prices, he no doubt set prices as low as was necessary to achieve £1m worth of sales. He, as much as anyone, has been responsible for the mess we are in."

The Sales Director was genuinely bewildered. He had, after all, been following, and following to the letter, Board urgings to try and get volume up at all costs (literally) and, within this mandate, he had been very successful. Like most people round a Board table, he was not a financial man. He left that to others. In the context of the general level of business understanding of the time it was not in any way his fault, nor indeed that of anyone else round the Board table, who had set the mandate in the first place.

Fortunately he rapidly accepted the need for the different "margin" approach, although it would substantially add to his burdens, for product would be much more difficult to sell. The subsequent success of the company tells its own story.

What Level of Gross Margin Percentage should be aimed for?

(1) Ignoring cash and service companies like banks and supermarkets, most manufacturing companies achieving less than about 25% gross margin are likely to fail sooner or later, and the lower the margin, the sooner it will fail.

(2) Companies begin to achieve real strength, cash flow, and financial durability, because of the comparatively good "real" income, once margins get over about 40%. And

(3) The real high-flyers, like properly structured electronics companies, begin to get into their stride at over 60%.

There is an apocryphal story about Sir Ernest Harrison, Chairman and Managing Director of The Racal Electronics Group, who one year was heard to complain that competition in a certain sector of the market was so fierce that "just to show how bad it is, margins have been forced down to under 80%".

Successful *v* Unsuccessful Management

It cannot have been quite like this, but the remark illustrates the point about management gut-feel and about the attitudes that mark out the successful businessman, the successful management team, from the unsuccessful.

Chapter V

"VULNERABLE" v "SAFE" BUSINESSES

Same Real Income at Widely Differing Sales Levels

In Chapter III the following figures were derived from the gross margin percentages to produce £100 of gross margin:

Figure 8

Company	Fixed Costs £	GM %	Sales for Breakeven £
A	100	5%	2,000
B	100	10%	1,000
C	100	20%	500
D	100	25%	400
E	100	30%	334
F	100	40%	250
G	100	50%	200

to which may be added:

H	100	60%	167
I	100	70%	143
J	100	80%	125
K	100	90%	111
L	100	100%	100

Notice how widely the sales levels vary, from £2,000 at one end of the scale to just £100 at the other, a mere 1/20th. *All* produce the same gross margin, the same *real* income.

If the same exercise is attempted another way round on the following figures, the answer to the first is clearly a (loss) of (£2,500), namely 25% of the £10,000 sales shortfall below breakeven of £20,000:

Figure 9

MONTHLY PROFIT/(LOSS)
Company 1 Breakeven £20,000 Gross Margin 25%

	£		£
Sales	10,000	Profit/(Loss)	(2,500)
Sales	20,000	Profit/(Loss)	?
Sales	50,000	Profit/(Loss)	?
Sales	100,000	Profit/(Loss)	?

Company 2 Breakeven £50,000 Gross Margin 10%

	£		£
Sales	10,000	Profit/(Loss)	?
Sales	20,000	Profit/(Loss)	?
Sales	50,000	Profit/(Loss)	?
Sales	100,000	Profit/(Loss)	?

Company 3 Breakeven £10,000 Gross Margin 50%

	£		£
Sales	10,000	Profit/(Loss)	?
Sales	20,000	Profit/(Loss)	?
Sales	50,000	Profit/(Loss)	?
Sales	100,000	Profit/(Loss)	?

Answers

Figure 10

MONTHLY PROFIT OR (LOSS)
Company 1 Breakeven £20,000 Gross Margin 25%

Sales	10,000	(Loss)	(2,500)
Sales	20,000	—	Breakeven
Sales	50,000	Profit	7,500
Sales	100,000	Profit	20,000

Company 2 Breakeven £50,000 Gross Margin 10%

Sales	10,000	(Loss)	(4,000)
sales	20,000	(Loss)	(3,000)
Sales	50,000	—	Breakeven
Sales	100,000	Profit	5,000

Company 3 Breakeven £10,000 Gross Margin 50%

Sales	10,000	—	Breakeven
Sales	20,000	Profit	5,000
Sales	50,000	Profit	20,000
Sales	100,000	Profit	45,000

The "Most Vulnerable" version of the Company
Company 2 is clearly accident prone. However good the market, up to quite high levels of turnover it loses money or breaks even. And above breakeven profits are small.

The "Fairly-Vulnerable" version
Company 1 is much less accident prone, although still with a tendency to make losses in a particularly bad market, but with *four times* the capacity to make good profits in a buoyant market.

The "Least-Vulnerable" version
Company 3, however, seems proof against all adversity, however poor its sales; conversely, given only small encouragement from the market, really good profits begin to emerge.

The Overhead (£5,000) and Real Income at Breakeven of all three companies is in fact exactly the same, namely £5,000 (25% of 20 = 5; 10% of 50 = 5; 50% of 10 = 5). **The only difference lies in their Gross Margin Percentages.**

Scale of the Difference
It may not be easy at first to grasp the full significance of what is being said here:
- (a) Company 3 needs only *one-fifth* of the turnover of Company 2 to get the stability of breakeven point.
- (b) Company 3 produces *nine times* as much profit at £100,000 turnover as Company 2.
- (c) Conversely, whereas Company 2 is heavily in loss at £20,000 turnover, Company 1 at least breaks-even and Company 3 produces a useful profit, £5,000; as much profit as Company 2 at £100,000 turnover.

There can be little doubt which mode of operation you should aim for. Force up margins, be quite content to see volume drop away and aim for Company 3 if you possibly can, or at least avoid 2 at all costs. Remember the *only* difference in these three companies lies in their gross margin percentages. All have identical overheads and are therefore identical in size.

Typical Monthly Profit & Loss Account
Let's begin to incorporate some of the principles of the last few chapters into a formalised set of monthly management accounts. First, the Profit and Loss Account. Here, produced say within five days of the end of the month, is an Actual Profit and Loss Account compared with Budget:

Figure 11

XYZ LIMITED. PROFIT AND LOSS ACCOUNT FOR THE MONTH OF X

		Actual £'000	Budget £'000
1.	**Sales**	45	25
2.	Cost of Sales (Materials, Labour)	(40)	(16)
3.	**Gross Margin**	5	9
4.	Overheads	(12)	(8)
5.	**Profit/(Loss)**	(7)	1
6.	**Monthly Order Intake**	80	35
7.	**Closing Order Book**	55	60

Look firstly at whether, because the figures have been so quickly prepared, they are sufficiently accurate. Two features stand out:

(1) Gross margin of only £5,000 was earned on sales of £45,000. The Budget predicts nearly twice as much on half the sales, so the Actual should have been nearly four times better.

(2) Overheads, which are broadly "fixed" in nature, should not have "moved" much, but they have in fact increased by 50 per cent.

So both areas would be subject to more detailed enquiry:

(a) to establish their general accuracy;

(b) if accurate, to uncover just what *has* gone wrong in each area.

Supposing on further examination the figures are found to be sufficiently accurate, within a thousand pounds or so. Unknowledgeable management would be cock-a-hoop at the result. Sales are nearly twice budget, order intake over twice. The company is going like a bomb.

And likely to finish like a bomb. The clues are given by inserting two further lines in the accounts:

Figure 11a

		Actual	Budget
8.	**Gross Margin Percentage** (Line 3 divided by Line 1)	11%	36%
9.	**Breakeven** (Line 4 divided by Line 8)	108	22

36

Budgeted Results

What matters is not absolute sales but the *gap* between sales and breakeven. What should have happened, per the budget, is that sales should have been £3,000 better than the breakeven point of £22,000, giving a £1,000 profit (36% of £3,000).

Order intake at £35,000 should have been £13,000 better than breakeven, representing 1 1/2 months safe operation (i.e. at breakeven) or giving a profit of £5,000 (36% of £13,000) if the whole amount were to be despatched in a single month. Similarly, closing orders in hand should have represented nearly three months' work at breakeven. All in all, a comfortable, balanced, secure, well-run, if unambitious, company.

What actually happened was a shambles.

Actual Results

Sales were only £45,000 against a breakeven of £108,000, representing a *loss* of £7,000 (11% of £63,000).

The monthly order intake of £80,000 represented only three weeks operation at breakeven and the closing order book only two weeks operation at breakeven.

Working Capital Requirement

We will discuss shortly the other sting in the tail. For the moment it is sufficient to note that the working capital requirement of a company typically runs at approximately three months' sales (to finance stocks and debtors). So another £60,000 would have had to be found to support actual sales. A total of £135,000 was needed compared with £75,000 budgeted. Hardly a bankable proposition for a loss-making company.

Failure

In fact this actual company, which thought it was doing so well, was within a few weeks of hitting the ground. It only avoided it thanks to very rapid intervention.

The Reason for Failure

What happened was that in reducing prices to stimulate volume, management did not realise they were pushing up the breakeven point by far more than the increase in sales. The gap which should have been favourable at £3,000 ended up £63,000 the other way.

This is of course what happened to BMC and is precisely what has happened to many other companies. It may, at this very moment, be happening to you, with the consequence that you are either in active trouble, or you are not making the profit you should, which is the other side of the coin. Even if you are comfortably profitable already, significantly more might be possible.

Continuation

The next five chapters are devoted to the all-important question of Cash Flow, returning to the absorbing subject of sales pricing from Chapter XII onwards.

Chapter VI

CASH FLOW

Importance
Now for the key subject of cash flow. Cash is to a business what blood is to a living body. Allow it to drain away and the body becomes weak and sickly and eventually dies. The more cash can be generated, through healthy margins, and regenerated, by ploughing back profits into future product and market potential, the more healthy the company becomes. So rapid generation, conservation and effective utilisation of cash is the whole foundation on which a business rests. It is its very "life-blood". One aptly speaks of the "haemorrhaging" of a company, when the reverse is happening and cash is draining out unstemmed.

Profit Actively Misleading
Unfortunately, all too often the concept of profit does not accurately reflect cash flow. For instance profit is struck, according to accepted accounting conventions, after valuing closing stock. This, and therefore "profits", can be improved, quite arbitrarily, by "allocating costs to stock", so helping to conceal, however unintentionally, any cash flow imbalances building up.

Suppose a company wins a £100,000 contract, which will take six months to get out of the door, priced as follows:

Figure 12

A TYPICAL CONTRACT

	£
Sales value	100,000
Less: Labour + Materials	60,000
Gross margin	40,000
Less: Overheads	30,000
Profit	10,000

Every month, under accepted accounting conventions, all labour and material costs incurred on the job will not show as a cost in the monthly profit and loss account but will be transferred out until the job is finished. A fair proportion of overhead may similarly be transferred out, making the situation, cosmetically, still better.

Thus in month one, despite £10,000 labour and material cost being incurred and £5,000 of overhead, the management accounts (if available at all) might show:

Figure 13

PROFIT AND LOSS ACCOUNT—MONTH ONE

	£		£
Sales	Nil		
Opening stock (direct cost content)	Nil		
Materials	6,000		
Labour	4,000		
Less: Closing stock (direct cost content)	(10,000)		
Cost of sales	Nil		
Gross margin	Nil		
Opening stock (overhead content)	Nil		Nil
Overheads	5,000	or	5,000
Less: Closing stock (overhead content)	(3,000)		(5,000)
Apparent Overheads	2,000		Nil
Profit (loss)	(2,000)		Nil

The figures in the boxes may or may not be separately shown in the accounts.

Faced with these figures, management's reaction is almost bound to be:

> "We are breaking even or only making a small loss, so no dangerous haemorrhaging here". A stock figure of £13,000 to £15,000 suddenly appears in the Balance Sheet ("whatever a Balance Sheet is"). "Marvellous" might be the reaction.

In month 2, again the company will show similar results and this time stock will be twice as "good". In month 3, the position will be even "better". And so on for 5 months.

Cash Drain is in Fact Frightening

In reality cash is draining out of the company at a rate of £15,000 per month. If not very adequately catered for, well in advance, the drain will rapidly overwhelm the company.

The Drain Continues even when the Contract is "Completed"

The problem is not solved even when the contract is completed and delivered, despite contrary appearances. Month six's profit and loss account will look spectacular:

Figure 14

PROFIT AND LOSS ACCOUNT—MONTH SIX

	£		£
Sales	100,000		
Opening stock (direct cost content)	50,000		
Materials	6,000		
Labour	4,000		
Closing stock (direct cost content)	(Nil)		
Cost of sales	60,000		
Gross margin	40,000		
Opening stock (overhead content)	15,000		25,000
Overheads	5,000	or	5,000
Closing stock (overhead content)	(Nil)		(Nil)
Apparent Overheads	20,000		30,000
Profit (loss)	20,000		10,000

To which the reaction will be:

> "£100,000 turnover in the month! Profit £10,000 to £20,000! In a single month. We are going like a bomb."

And once again ending like a bomb for, even now, its most unlikely the customer will pay immediately on delivery. He may take two to three months, he may take six months, he may never pay, if he is not chased.

Again a sudden item "Debtors £115,000" (i.e. including 15% VAT) appears in the Balance Sheet:

> "Marvellous, an even better asset". And it will stay there month after month—"the longer the better" may be the attitude, "it gives a nice, warm, cosy feeling".

The Bank Manager

Anything but nice, warm and cosy will be your Bank Manager's reaction. You will have arranged perhaps a £30,000 overdraft at the outset:

> "I am told one should have at least *some* overdraft facility, just in case, but it is unlikely ever to be used, or used more than marginally. £30,000 is painful enough against the personal commitment of my house anyway".

Month three

Phone call.

> "Mr. X, could you come and see me? Your overdraft is up to the limit." Painful negotiations. Limit raised to £50,000. More security extracted.

Month five

Mounting calls from the suppliers. Payment demanded for goods already delivered or no more supplies. You must have the raw materials to complete the contract. You must pay the staff . . . So you write out the cheques.

Month five-and-a-half

Phone call from the Manager . . . You explain:

> "You must understand. I have this big £100,000 contract. It's nearly finished. Unless I can get it out of the door . . ."

> "Must have the cash to pay suppliers. Must pay the staff. Inland Revenue pressing . . . You would be reckless to let me down at this stage."

> "All you Bankers are the same, only provide an umbrella when it is not raining . . ."

"What do you mean NO?"

"I'll go bust."

"You *can't* let me down, not at this late hour."

"There's another contract just behind the first . . ."

"What about my house . . ."

C U R R U M P ! ! !

No Apparent Reason, from the Accounts, why the Company should have Failed

To the unknowledgable there is little sign of *any* of this in the accounts. The company is breaking-even, or only making small losses. A valuable asset is building up in the balance sheet. And of course, after despatch the position looks even better. The company is profitable, to the extent of £10,000, and has a £115,000 asset. All is sunniness and light.

An illustration of the truly devastating difference there can be between Cash Flow and Profit. A very large number of companies have been wiped out by this very factor. It is *the* most common cause of company failure, which, of course, has at its root the fact that management (and their advisers) do not sufficiently understand cash flow, whatever the appearances to the contrary.

The Moral

Plan what is going to happen well before you start and *don't* start unless you have the full finance shown to be needed.

Chapter VII

STOCK AND DEBTOR REQUIREMENT

Calculating Working Capital Requirements

There is a useful rule-of-thumb for assessing how much "working capital" is going to be needed to finance stocks and debtors. Suppose your turnover is pitched at regular delivery of £10,000 per month, to avoid the large, one-off, contract, £120,000 a year.

Debtors (what is owed by your Customers)

If the customer takes, say, one month to pay, at any one time debtors will be £11,500 (i.e. including 15% VAT). If two months, £23,000. If three months, £34,500.

Figure 15

So:

DEBTOR REQUIREMENT IN RELATION TO TURNOVER

$$1 \text{ month} = \frac{11{,}500}{120{,}000} = 9 \cdot 6\% \text{ of annual turnover}$$

$$2 \text{ months} = \frac{23{,}000}{120{,}000} = 19 \cdot 2\% \text{ of annual turnover}$$

$$3 \text{ months} = \frac{34{,}500}{120{,}000} = 28 \cdot 8\% \text{ of annual turnover}$$

$$4 \text{ months} = \frac{46{,}000}{120{,}000} = 38 \cdot 3\% \text{ of annual turnover}$$

and so on.

Note how rapidly the figure climbs as "collection" gets worse, which is where a large company can so unwarrantably damage a small company, incidentally, by not paying promptly or by holding out for "normal", say 90 day, credit terms.

Typical Time Scales

In practice you have to be very good at debt collection to achieve less than two months; that is, if £10,000 worth of goods is delivered in January, being able to collect the money in full before the end of February.

It can, in practice, take up to the end of March (3 months), to the end of April (4 months), or even longer, depending on how good your customer is in stalling you off and how reluctant you are to press for payment, perhaps out of fear of alienating a major, or possibly only, source of business.

Usually you can only be tough once you have the confidence to do so (formal reminder after 30 days, warning after 45, solicitor's letter after 50, court action after 60).

Deliberate Delay

When you are a young company, customers may well play on your vulnerability, knowing you have insufficient muscle to do much about it. There may even be something more sinister, a competitor, for instance, taking a convenient opportunity, presented to him on a plate, of putting you out of business virtually before you start.

Amount to Predict for Estimating Purposes

So you should start by working on the assumption that debtors will amount to at least 3 to 4 months sales (30% to 40% of annual turnover), hoping to get it down to 2 months (around 20%) within a year or two.

Stock

Next there is stock to consider. If the **raw material** content of sales is say, 40% and you need to keep at least 6 weeks' stock in hand, then raw material stocking requirements will be 40% of $6/52 = 5\%$ of annual turnover.

Then if you need to keep say 6 weeks' **work-in-progress** in hand, it will be equivalent say to another 1 month's sales, another 8% of annual turnover (work-in-progress being valued at say 70% of finished sales price). Similarly just over one month of **finished goods** stock needs to be added, another 8%.

Gross Current Asset Requirement (Stocks + Debtors)

Stocks, in round figures, may thus run at the equivalent of around 20% of turnover. So stocks and debtors combined require financing to the equivalent of between 40% to 60% of annual turnover or £40,000 to £60,000 for every £100,000 of turnover.

The Killer Trap Springs

The implications are truly daunting. It can be an entirely unseen factor, building up within your company and striking at the very moment success begins to be achieved. It may rear its head at the very moment orders and sales begin to forge ahead as you successfully strive to get turnover up past breakeven point as quickly as possible. It is *the* great killer. "The scorpion sting." The formative years of a company are the most vulnerable.

Further discussion on the acute funding and other problems this can give rise to is given in Chapter IX (Figure 28 on page 80 illustrates some of the difficulties).

The effects on trading can be Cataclysmic

Once the strain does begin to surface, it will show itself, at the very least, in suppliers starting to withhold deliveries of key material needed for production, which will hamper, perhaps seriously, your company's own efforts to get the product out of the door, to meet customer delivery deadlines and to bring in urgently needed cash flow. Management will find their time and energies increasingly being diverted into tense efforts to raise more finance. Even if further funding *is* successfully secured, it could take weeks to raise. Meanwhile, the distraction of time and effort could well divert management attention away from the operating side just long enough to allow a competitor into the field.

The competitor will have been attracted by the success of your product and will be just waiting for the opportunity to get a toe-hold in your market. His task will be much helped by the fact that, once your customers sense something is wrong (which they are almost *bound* to do) they will grow cautious about taking so much product from you and may even begin to look around for other sources. Mr. Peter Michael, who produces the hugely successful Quantel system, which squeezes, shrinks, and tumbles pictures on your TV screen (always assuming the set is properly adjusted) is on record as saying that sometimes in the electronics industry, say just before a major overseas exhibition where a new product is about to be launched, a mere 10 minutes lost in having the product ready on time and therefore missing the delivery arrangements can lose a whole market sector to the competition. Quantel are world leaders just because they have been able to meet what most companies would consider impossibly tight deadlines.

It's hard enough getting the technical side right on time. If financial restrictions are also holding a company back, even for a short time, it can do lasting damage. Unless the size of a company's working capital requirement is therefore very adequately forecast, catered for and controlled in advance, sooner or later the company is almost certain to plunge into this trap.

Creditors (what you owe your Suppliers)

There is one mitigating aspect. In just the same way as your customers can spin out having to pay you, you can spin out having to pay your suppliers for the raw material supplies you get from them on credit, the **trade creditors,** but the amounts are smaller.

A Smaller Factor

If you want to avoid Creditors getting tough to the point of taking *you* to Court and perhaps actually withholding supplies, you are unlikely to get away with more than 2 to 3 months delay in payment. Payment of some of your other costs, like wages and salaries, cannot be delayed, so a fairly relaxed level of creditors, including **"other creditors"** like owings for rent, VAT and PAYE, is unlikely to contribute more than around 13% of annual turnover towards funding stocks and debtors.

Total Net Current Asset Requirement (Stocks + Debtors − Creditors)

So the total looks roughly as follows:

Figure 16

CURRENT ASSET REQUIREMENT		
	No. of Months (Say)	% Annual Turnover
Debtors	2	19%
Stock:		
Raw Material	1½	5%
Work in Progress	1½	8%
Finished Goods	1	8%
Total Stocks		21%
Gross Current Assets		40%
Less: Creditors		
Trade	3	10%
Other	1	3%
Total Creditors		13%
Net Current Assets		27%

Thus, in a well run company the requirement can be at least 27% of annual turnover, say 3 to 3½ months' sales equivalent. In a poorly-run company, it may be up to twice as much.

Going back to the example given earlier, where it took six months to "complete" the contract and say a further six months to actually get paid, operating costs amounted to £15,000 per month (assuming follow-on orders). So the **Gross Current Asset** requirement was £180,000 (12 × £15,000) just for stocks and debtors. Trade creditors amounted to, say, three months' purchases of raw material £18,000 (3 × £6,000) and "other creditors" were, say, £5,000, equivalent to one month's overhead. Total creditors were therefore £23,000. Deduct this total from £180,000 and the **Net Current Asset** requirement was £157,000. No wonder the £30,000 overdraft only lasted 3 months, and £50,000 5 months. The company was undercapitalised by a factor of three!

Poor Control can escalate the Requirement rapidly

The small margin for error should be noted. 1 month's sales in a company with a turnover of say £½m p.a. amounts, with VAT, to £48,000, and of £1m to over £96,000. Neglect the cash flow side for just a few days, let alone weeks, and the company can be in serious difficulties almost before you know it.

The "swing" in the figures will be at least as frightening for your own company. So you should make a point of measuring the position regularly each month and certainly within not more than two weeks from the end of each month, taking immediate action where necessary if you want to be sure of staying out of the all-too-aptly named "cash black hole" or "cash sink".

The Bank Manager got it Wrong

In fact the Bank Manager in the example who granted the £30,000 facility and later raised it to £50,000, should have sensed management had little or no knowledge of cash flow, of the effects of a long term contract, or of the mechanics of business. He should have firmly declined to provide *any* bank support until he had sat down with you, made sure you did understand all the issues, and not agreed to help until a radically revised business plan was available, perhaps involving regular progress payments first being negotiated with the customer. Otherwise all he was doing was making the loss of your house and loss of your company a *certainty*. You both lost out. The Manager is going to be a good deal more cautious next time, perhaps starving someone who does know what he is doing from getting the funds he needs.

Another Dangerous Cash Flow Trap

Yet another deceiving feature can creep in here. Once you have drawn fully on all external sources of finance and have reached your overdraft limit, there is only one further source you can lean on, creditors. The only course left open to you is to delay payment to your suppliers beyond the agreed credit period of, say, 3 months. You will almost certainly be doing so without becoming fully aware of the extent to which it is happening.

Effective concealment quite inadvertently arises through the way the figures are grouped in conventional accounts. Because creditors are *deducted* from the gross figure, as creditors get *larger* and grow to the equivalent of, say, 20%, 30%, 40% etc. of annual turnover, the total net current asset requirement appears to get *smaller:*

Figure 17

EFFECT OF ESCALATING CREDITORS

	% Annual Turnover		
Gross Current Assets (say)	40%	40%	40%
Less: Normal Creditors	13%	13%	13%
Net Current Assets (as before)	27%	27%	27%
Less: Overdue Creditors	7%	17%	27%
***Apparent* Net Current Assets** to be financed	20%	10%	NIL

As the apparent requirement goes down, management are given the wholly misleading impression that the turnover-related funding requirement is *easing*, whereas the exact reverse is happening. By the time the pressures get sufficiently bad for the full gravity of the situation to become apparent, it can often be far too late to save the company.

Sudden End

For those who fail to understand, and therefore fail to identify, these stresses and strains building up deep within the company, the end, when it comes, will seem to come out of the blue. Suddenly a creditor or the bank will petition for winding-up for no really apparent reason. Why should it happen at that particular juncture? Matters seem no better and no worse than they have done for quite some time.

This leaves management badly mislead and bewildered and only too ready to cast around blaming just about every cause except the right one. For instance that it is "all the Bank Manager's fault for not lending more". Whereas, as just shown, the Manager went far further than he should and was fundamentally misguided in his support of the company. Perhaps *his* knowledge of business was not as good as it should have been either.

Incidentally Bank Managers who do not fully understand the key cash flow, margin and other issues set out in this book, risk lending either too much to a given company in a given situation, or too little, with possibly most damaging consequences for both sides, as will perhaps be appreciated.

Creditor Strain

A convenient way to avoid the problem of failure to detect the cash flow strains building up as they happen is to measure "**creditor strain**" each month. Creditor strain is the money value of the "overdue" element shown in Figure 17 above.

In the absence of having a specific "aged list" of creditors to guide you (a monthly list of what you owe, aged into the months in which the liability was first incurred), the "normal" level of creditors can approximately be found by totalling, say, the last three months' purchases of raw material, and adding part or all of the current month's overheads (to cover VAT, PAYE, etc.), as was done in arriving at the creditors figure of £23,000 on Page 49. This is then deducted from total creditors to isolate the strain element.

The trend in build-up of creditor strain from month to month will then give you a true feel for the real cash flow pressures building up within the business, hopefully in time for you to head-off the danger.

Thus if the company in question had had actual creditors of £72,000, the strain element would be £49,000, equivalent to an extra 8 months supply of raw materials.

"Net Creditor Strain"

For full effect, the extent to which the overdraft is over, or under, the limit should be added to, or subtracted from, the creditor strain figure to give Net Creditor Strain.

If companies deliberately lean on their creditors to keep their overdraft and therefore interest bill low, but there is sufficient slack in the facility to enable creditors to be paid should they become pressing, that is an entirely different matter. The company *does* have the resources to pay.

The net creditor strain figure, after allowing for this cushion, if any, in the overdraft, therefore measures true strain, the extent to which the company cannot pay even if it wants to . . .

The often quite Unintentional Harm one Company can do to Another, particularly a Larger Company to a Smaller, by Slow Payment

One company's creditor is, of course, another company's debtor. You may already have spotted the inherent inconsistency of assuming *you* need not pay your bills for 3 months, yet expect to collect what you are owed within 2 months.

Every percentage point by which you allow your creditors to creep up will, of course, impose financial burdens of like amount on your suppliers.

However, a big company, with plenty of financial muscle and above all a full and proper understanding of cash flow, can take such movements in its stride. On the other hand a small company without such muscle *and particularly without adequate cash flow understanding*, may be quite unwarrantably harmed by such action, perhaps not even appreciating the dangers until it is too late.

Be very careful, therefore, that in quite properly husbanding cash through slow payment of creditors, you do not in the process damage, perhaps irrevocably, a vital source of supply or technical ingenuity on which you may crucially depend. How often have you heard a company complain "We can't understand it. Quite suddenly one of our key suppliers has gone bust without any warning, leaving production totally disrupted. It will take *months* to organise satisfactory alternatives" (particularly if there is no other UK source). "How inconsiderate."

Inadvertent Armageddon

It rarely seems to cross their minds that *they* have probably caused it, through over-hard bargaining on price (affecting margins) and in delayed payment. Incidentally, the relatively small number of key executives in big business who *do* fully understand cash flow often do not seem to realise how widespread is the general lack of understanding of such issues in the UK. They may therefore have insufficient sense of the dangers that tough-minded business methods can create for their (weaker) brethren.

Conversely you can very much help a bright, struggling young operation to get successfully off the ground (which after all, all companies once were, including even your own!) by being perhaps over-prompt on payment, at least to selected clearly identified cases, making payment, say, within a few days of delivery. The effect can be quite disproportionaly beneficial to the supplier, as hopefully this discussion has shown.

Payment Systems

Most big companies have formalised, computer-based, payment systems with built-in time scales of their own (often intentionally!). Miss a delivery or fail to get an invoice into the system on time and a whole month may elapse before the next processing cycle takes place, which itself may take 2-3 weeks.

So any accelerated help given to suppliers may need special arrangements to be made to pre-empt the normal payment system, and should be organised well in advance.

Detecting Creditor Harm from Published Accounts

The cash flow discussion in this chapter assumes a "normal" level of creditors of, say, 13%, being 10% "trade" and 3% "other". These are very rough ballpark figures. Each company will have its own more specific figures (based on the actual raw material content of sales and number of months credit given).

Broadly, however, an indication of how much a company is "leaning" on its suppliers can quickly be established from its annual audited accounts, by dividing trade creditors by annual turnover. If the figure is substantially above, say, 10% (allowing, however, for the fairly rare special cases, where, for good reason, the figures may well be different) the company may be causing its suppliers to suffer quite unwarrantably and perhaps quite unintentionally from slow payment, with evident dangers.

Debtor Control Format

A useful monthly layout to control DEBTORS is as follows:

Figure 18

XYZ LIMITED DEBTORS (INCLUDING VAT) AS AT END NOVEMBER (£'000)

	Dec	Nov	Oct	Sept	Aug	Prior	Total	Days
Aug					[15·3]	12·3	27·6	71
					100%			
Sept				[13·1]	13·0	1·6	27·7	59
				100%	85%			
Oct			[16·9]	10·1	4·1	—	31·1	63
			100%	77%	27%			
Nov		[21·9]	11·5	0·5	—	—	33·9	52
		100%	68%	4%				
Dec	[ ]							

Total debtors at the end of November were £33,900, of which £21,900 represented invoicings for November (1 month); £11,500 remained uncollected from October (2 months); £500 from September (3 months). December's invoicings will be inserted in the December [box], the amount left from November will be inserted under the £21,900, and so on, with total debtors outstanding at the end of December being inserted in the Total column.

The percentages are calculated downwards on the original month's invoicings (£11,500 is 68% of £16,900 etc.), which then shows progress each month in collecting 1 month, 2 month, 3 month, etc. debtors.

1 month debtors in September were 85% of August invoicings, in October 77% of September invoicings, and in November 68% of October invoicings, indicating progressive improvement.

Similarly two month debtors were down from 27% in October to a mere 4% in November, an excellent performance.

Any laxity in collecting debts shows up clearly in the earlier columns, which are therefore a useful indicator of possible bad debts building up.

"Days" Calculation

It will be remembered that on page 45 it was said you have to be very good at debt collection to achieve better than 2 months. To show actual achievement, a "days" column is inserted. It is calculated as follows: at the end of November, total debtors of £33,900 represent how many "days"?:

Figure 18a

CALCULATION OF NOVEMBER DAYS		
	£'000	
Total Debtors	33·9	
Deduct November invoicings	21·9	= 30 days
Balance	12·0	
As this is less than the October invoicings of 16·9, take the proportion $^{12·0}/_{16·9}$ of October's 31 days = 71% of 31		= 22 days
	Total	52 As above

Again the Days column in the example given in table 18 indicates rapid improvement in debt collection. It also indicates that 52 days is about the limit of what is feasible for a company whose stated trading terms are "30 days net".

Self-Correcting Control

The importance of this schedule lies in the fact that the debt collection staff who prepare it know that any slippages are bound to raise adverse comment when seen by management. So they tend to take action on their own account, ringing round to all customers to chase up what they owe, *before* the accounts are submitted to management. In course of time customers get so used to, or fed-up with, being chased at around the same time each month, they programme earlier payment into their systems.

If this exercise *has* to be done very promptly after the month end in order to meet tight deadlines for getting management accounts to management, "control" becomes very prompt. Apart from bringing in cash more quickly, it will also significantly reduce the possibility of bad debts. The company is led to act before too much time has elapsed, can cut off further deliveries and can take early legal action, hopefully before the customer risks finally running out of money. It becomes a valuable *self-correcting* mechanism.

Creditor Control

Creditors can of course be shown in the same fashion, although here a company will be at pains not to pay too quickly on one hand nor too slowly on the other!

Conclusion

In summary, a typical, tightly controlled, manufacturing company will need to arrange funding of around £27,000 for every £100,000 of annual turnover, just to finance that turnover itself. In a badly controlled company it could well be double, up to £50,000 for every £100,000. Above all, turn your back on control and let it slip for a mere period of days let alone weeks and the requirement can escalate frighteningly and even rapidly overwhelm the company.

Chapter VIII

CASH FLOW FORECASTING AND CONTROL

This Chapter, and Chapters IX and X go to the very heart of running a business successfully. To obtain full benefit, you might like to work through, and master, the Cash Flow format given in the Appendix, page 169 onwards, before reading further.

Frequent, Reasonably Accurate, Management Information Seems the Key Characteristic of Successful Companies

A striking feature of nearly all successful companies is how quickly and how regularly actual performance is checked against budget. In GEC key figures from all 250 reporting units in the Group are on Lord Weinstock's desk within 21 days of the end of each month and will of course have been seen well before then by the MDs of the operating units themselves —sales, order intake, output, staff numbers, productive hours, stocks, debtors, despatches, etc. *That* is why GEC is so successful. Very few companies that have gone bust or just generally got into trouble in the recessions of the past few years have had effective budgeting and financial control systems. Very few of those who have survived and done well have not.

The reason is straightforward: **These systems are effectively the mirror-image of management's own perception of business. The better you understand, the faster you want key information, in a certain form. The less you understand, the less you see the need for it.**

The Fund the author runs, which was set up in 1979, thought it was chancing its arm in insisting on a 14 day deadline for getting out monthly accounts. But once management acquire a full feel for what the accounts are showing they tend to say:

"What's all this about a 14 day deadline?".

We explain that we think it only reasonable, muttering about "well-run company," "matter of professionalism" and so on. To which the reaction so often is:

"Forget 14 days. We need the information in 2 or 3".

"It's far too dangerous to wait any longer".

We know, then, that the business lessons have fully gone home and we can sit back and relax (figuratively speaking).

Cash Flow Format

Set out in the Appendix to this book is a Profit and Loss Account and Cash Flow format developed in the early 70's and now the foundation of financial control and business insight within the companies supported by the present Fund. It has been used in a wide variety of companies, in this and earlier forms, for the best part of 10 to 15 years. Its main purpose is to place at the fingertips of management a simple, effective, complete and immediate form of day to day financial planning and control.

The Budgeting Process—Business Plan

Well-run companies will, at the start of each financial year, draw up a *budget* or *business plan*. The budget effectively targets performance for the coming year. Actual performance is *monitored* as soon as possible after the month (or week) end. Divergences are *"fed back"* to *control* the performance of the company and head it onto target.

"Control" means a precise system of measurement that remains accurate as the company expands, without inhibiting or retarding that expansion, so long as it is proceeding soundly. It is a "dynamic" form of control that can rapidly adapt to changing conditions within a company and yet still remain fully effective, not "static" control in the sense of rigidly pegging everything back to a pre-determined level, regardless of circumstances.

There is a close analogy to be drawn here with the way a guided missile can be *made* to hit its target, in contrast for instance to a bullet or shell, which will only do so if correctly aimed *before* it is fired. In the latter case, the target will only be hit, after the shell has left the barrel, if the target's movement is *predictable*. In the former, however, the target can still be hit even if its movement is completely random and unpredictable, indeed positively evasive. So with the art of using dynamics correctly to target a company's cash flow and "home" its operation onto target.

Cause of Divergences

1. If the budget is unsoundly based, it will not reflect the true dynamics of the company and will therefore form an inadequate bench mark against which to compare and target actual performance

or

2. Actual performance itself is worse than it should be.

Identifying the Real Dynamic
It is not until a sufficient number of previous month's actual results have been built up and studied that the real dynamics of a company can be identified. Only then can a budget be structured that reflects those same dynamics, one that does accurately reflect the real trends of events going on within the business. Only then, in turn, can you evolve a creditable *business plan*, certain of its reliability.

Correct Dynamic Ensures Correct Forecasting
Only a budget that *does* accurately reflect the way a company is behaving at the moment will be able to *forecast* accurately where it is heading, assuming that the basic factors governing its behaviour remain unchanged. What, however, if the basic factors are heading the company in a wrong direction, which they may well be?

Consciously Changing the Dynamic
If the basic factors are not favourable the dynamic needs to be consciously changed to one that is both attainable, given sufficient effort, and one that will lead the company into the improved performance desired.

The second stage of the process consists of driving the company into this new mould, exerting "control" month by month.

Accuracy of Cash Flow Forecasts
If the correct dynamic is accurately reflected in the budget, it will not matter if market and other conditions change between the time the budget is prepared and subsequent performance. The *cash flow* targeting should still be accurate as the discussion towards the end of this Chapter will explain. It is cash flow, of course, at the end of the day that is being targeted and needs to be adhered to, at a pre-determined level.

Form of Cash Flow
It will be seen from the format given at the Appendix that there are 14 columns. The first column gives the actuals for the month before the start of the new financial year. The final 12 columns give the budget for the 12 months. The actual result of the first of those 12 months is then inserted to the left of the 12 columns, next to the starting Actual. As the year progresses the first month's budget is replaced by the second month's actuals, and so on. Only *one* column of figures needs to be updated each month.

The effect is to build up actual performance to the left, whilst the budget runs off to the right. At the interface, actual progress is compared with budget for the particular month in question.

Figure 19

MONTHLY "PERCEPTION AND CONTROL" FORMAT
CASH FLOW £'000

		Actual		Budget
		Last Month	This Month	This Month
Ref.	**Current Assets Per Balance Sheet**			
(30/31)	Debtors	50 (60 days)	130 (138 days)	60 (78 days)
(32/34)	Stock [Line 10]	105 (198 days)	120 (90 days)	80 (150 days)
(36)	**Gross Current Assets**	155	250	140
(39)	Less: Creditors	85 (111 days)	150 (150 days)	80 (111 days)
(40)	**Net Current Assets**	70	100	60

Cash Flow in Month

(41)	Increase (Decrease) NCA [Per 40]		30 [100−70]	(10) [60−70]
(42)	Capital Expenditure		10	—
(44)	**Gross Cash Flow Out(In)**		40	(10)
	Deduct (Add) contribution from:			
(45)	Pre-Tax Profits/(Losses) [Line 18/22]		(7)	1
(46)	Depreciation [As included in line 17]		2	2
(48)	**Cash Profits/(Losses)**		(5)	3
(49)	**Net Cash Flow Out(In)**		45	(13)

Per Balance Sheet

(56/57)	**Closing Overdraft** [Per 49]	48	93 [48+45]	35 [48−13]
	(Limit 50)			

Net Creditor Strain

	3 Months Purchases (5)	70	90	66
	Less Actual Creditors (39)	85	150	80
	Creditor (Strain) Ease	(15)	(60)	(14)
	Bank (Strain) Ease (56)	2	(43)	15
	Net (Strain) Ease	(13)	(103)	1

Figure 20

MONTHLY "PERCEPTION AND CONTROL" FORMAT
PROFIT AND LOSS ACCOUNT £'000

		Actual			Budget
		Prior Month	Last Month	This Month	This Month
Ref.					
(1)	**Sales**	24	20	45	25
	Cost of Sales				
(4)	Opening Stock	70	80	105	75
(5)	Purchases	20	30	40	16
(6)	Labour	4	11	15	5
(10)	(Closing Stock)	(80)	(105)	(120)	(80)
(11)	**Cost of Sales**	14	16	40	16
(12)	**Gross Margin**	10	4	5	9
(17)	**Overheads**	8	10	12	8
(18/22)	**Profit/(Loss)**	2	(6)	(7)	1

Key Data

(23)	**Gross Margin %** (12÷1)	42%	20%	11%	36%
(24)	**Breakeven** (17÷23)	19	50	108	22
(25)	**Order Intake in Month**	10	10	80	35
(27)	**Orders in Hand Month-end**	35	20	55	60

"Quick" Profit/(Loss)

Sales (1)		24	20	45	25
Breakeven (24)		19	50	108	22
Over (Under)		5	(30)	(63)	3
GM% (23)		42%	20%	11%	36%
P(L)		2	(6)	(7)	1

61

Build Up of Actuals

The build up of actual performance to the left, once sufficient months have elapsed, begins to identify the real dynamics of the company: gross margin percentage, overhead level, breakeven level, build-up of orders and sales, ratio of debtors to sales, stock to cost of sales, creditors to purchases.

As such factors become ever more accurately identified, you can constantly update the budget as the months go by, progressively refining it to reflect these same dynamics ever more accurately. You then have at your fingertips an ever more accurate way of determining where the company is *really* heading.

To illustrate the principles involved, let's go back and expand the Cash Flow and Profit and Loss Account illustrations used in Chapter V, producing figures 19 and 20 respectively. (The line reference numbers are the same as those used in the Appendix where a fuller description of the way to compile cash flows is set out.)

Net Current Asset Requirement

Line (40) is a reflection of the Net Current Asset requirement discussed in Chapter VII. As discussed on page 48 the Net Current Asset figure for a particular month, budget and actual, should total broadly 27% of annual turnover, roughly the last three month's sales.

Looking at the make-up of the total Net Current Asset figure, debtors should roughly total the last two months sales; stock (raw material + work in progress + finished goods) should total broadly two and a quarter months; and creditors should total say one and a half month's sales. **These levels are rough guides. You will, in course of time, evolve more precise figures for your own business.**

"Days" Calculation

The "days" figures inserted in figure 19 are derived from the Profit and Loss Account (Figure 20) in the way shown in Figure 21:

Significance of the "Days" figures—Debtors

It is at once apparent that actual debtors at 138 days are 60 days more than the 78 days budgeted. Going further, it can be argued that the budget itself is unsound. Collection *should* be tighter, say 60 days. In which case actual performance is 78 days slack. Another £65,000 *should* have been collected (24+41).

Figure 21

CALCULATION OF "DAYS"

	Actual			Budget
	Prior Month	Last Month	This Month	This Month

Stock

divide Closing Stock	(10)	80	105	120	80
by Cost of Sales	(11)	14	16	40	16
=No. Months		5·7	6·6	3·0	5·0
=Days (× 30)		171	198	90	150

Debtors

Sales (1) This Month	20	45	25
Last Month	24	20	20
Prior Month	6 (part)	24	15 (part) = 15/24
Balance earlier	—	41	—
Total Debtors (30/31)	50	130	60
=No. Months	2·0	4·6 (Say)	2·6
=Days	60	138	78

Creditors

Purchases (5) This Month	30	40	16
Last Month	20	30	30
Prior Month	20 (Say)	20	20
Sub Total	70	90	66
Balance over 3 Months	15	60	14
Total Creditors (39)	85	150	80
=No. Months	3·7 (Say)	5·0 (Say)	3·7 (Say)
=Days	111	150	111

Stock "Days"

Stocks *should* be around 70 days, 2¼ times £40,000 (this month's cost of sales (11)) or £90,000. The actual level of £120,000 should have been lower by £30,000. Furthermore the budget should have been pitched at around £36,000 (2¼ ×16) not £80,000, again an indication of thoroughly weak-minded budgeting.

Creditor "Days"

The same exercise can be done with the creditors figures. 111 days looks about right for last month and for the budget, but clearly creditor strain of £60,000 has built up in the current month, equivalent to, say, 2 months over the acceptable 3-month norm. All the danger signals are flashing, as shown by the net creditor strain calculation at the foot of Figure 19. (Note how this ties in with the calculations in Figure 21.)

These "days" calculations need only be approximate, but they do pin down with great precision where the net current asset requirement *should* lie in any given situation. You are quite unable to do this from the form of conventional cash flow, incidentally. It is a major weakness with the conventional form (one of several such weaknesses).

Cash Flow Proper

With this form of presentation, **cash flow reduces down to just three aspects. The increase (decrease) in the month of the:**

(1) **Net current asset requirement** (41).
(2) **Capital expenditure** (plant, buildings, etc.) (42).
(3) **Losses to be financed** (48).

Ease of Understanding

The purpose is to produce the clearest possible concept to put across to a non-financial board, the Sales Director, the Production Director, the R & D Director and their teams. Cash Flow is the very heart of a business. It *is* the business, as we have seen.

Depreciation

There is a slight complication in the treatment of depreciation. The profit and loss result (18/22) will have been arrived at after charging depreciation as a cost.

Depreciation, however, is not a real cash cost. It is only a notional monthly charge inserted to reflect the use of an asset, bought some time before (42). Thus plant may be depreciated at 10% per year, vehicles at 25% per year i.e. over 4 years, and so on.

Declared losses at (18/22) have been artificially increased by this notional charge. The effect needs to be removed to arrive at true cash loss. This month's loss of £7,000 is overstated, in cash terms, by £2,000. So £2,000 has to be "added back" (46). The CASH LOSS is thus only £5,000, as shown at (48). Equally, declared profits *increase* when depreciation is added back, per the budget column. (For fuller treatment, please see e.g. Stage XVII, page 174 of the Appendix.)

Stock Errors have no Effect on Cash Flow

Any other non-cash item in the cash flow must be treated similarly. This raises a fascinating point. *Stock errors are a non-cash item.* If there is an error in stock (10) which of course equals (32/34), the same error will affect profit or loss (45) by the same amount. Stock *overstated* by £10,000 will *increase* profits by £10,000. Stock *understated* by £10,000 will *reduce* profits by £10,000.

The two features cancel out for cash flow purposes, as indeed they must. Non-cash items cannot possibly affect cash flow. The net cash flow (49) is entirely unaffected. This equally applies to the effect of taking overheads out of stock and basing all stock figures just on labour and material content only, as is done in the format given in the Appendix (to preserve accurate margins). Most conventional accounts include an artificial book-keeping adjustment to take account of "overheads" as was shown in Chapter VI. Removing this overhead content in stock *cannot* affect cash flow.

Cash Flow (49) is the Key Figure to Monitor

"It pays the wages on Friday". Or not as the case may be. A net outflowing of cash has to come from somewhere, either increased borrowings (56/57) or by running up creditors (39). The Bank Manager will be monitoring the former, relentlessly. The net-creditor-strain calculation will be red-flagging the latter, warning you of the implications of a steadily—or perhaps not so steadily—rising trend.

Effect of Profits

Whereas cash *losses* cause an increase in the net requirement at (49), *profits* help to finance it and therefore *reduce* it. This is demonstrated in the budget column.

Profits only a Small Cash Flow Item

The striking feature of cash flow behaviour is that in most companies cash profit (48) is nearly always quite small in relation to the much bigger cash flow swings occuring on account of capital expenditure (42) and particularly on account of the net current asset requirement (41).

"Budgets are not Worth the Paper they are Written on"

Another thought-provoking point. You will often hear it said: "budgets are not worth the paper they are written on. They are out of date almost from the day the ink is dry on the paper".

Why? "Because no sales forecast is accurate even days after it is first made". True. "So no cash flow forecast can possibly be accurate." Untrue.

Untrue?

Any one who makes the claim that "cash flow cannot possibly be accurate because the sales forecasts on which they are based can never be accurate" *fundamentally misunderstands cash flow*.

It is a dangerous misunderstanding, for it may divert management attention away from an attempt even being made to control the company properly. The production of well-structured budgets and the careful monitoring of actual progress against them, which is the only way to exercise really effective control, may then not take place at all. Or it may only take place in a very half hearted manner. In the latter case it is likely to be largely or wholly ineffective, little if any confidence being placed in the reliability of the process.

Where is the Fallacy in this Apparent Paradox?

Failure to achieve projected sales may indeed result in profits being less than budgeted. Cash contributions for profits will then indeed be less, and cash flow will indeed be poorer on that account.

However as we have already said **profits are only likely to be a comparatively minor factor in cash flow** anyway. *After-tax* profits in even the most spectacularly successful company will rarely run at more than about 10% of annual turnover and most companies will operate at well below this figure, say, 7% or 8% *before* tax.

The other, overwhelmingly major, factor is of course the net current asset requiremment. It too is turnover related. In a well-controlled company, it will drop if sales drop and increase if sales increase, in line with the 27% rule discussed in Chapter VII.

Lower Turnovers help Cash Flow

So if turnover falls, cash flow should actually improve! Marvellous. In one company the author handled, turnover for a particular year was £4m down on budget. A loss of £½m resulted instead of a profit of £½m. Did it matter? Not to the cash requirement. Closing overdraft was only £10,000 adrift from the budget of £3m. Why? Reduced net current asset requirement produced £1m improvement in cash flow (27% of £4m), exactly compensating for the adverse swing in profits. Here is an example of how "a company making a loss can sometimes have a stronger, more positive, cash flow, than one making a profit, absurd as it may seem" as first mentioned in Chapter I.

Rapid Expansion

In rapidly growing companies, however, "cash flow rapidly goes out of the window as the company expands" (Walter Goldsmith former Director General of the Institute of Directors) for the very opposite reason.

"Overtrading"

The really dangerous situation arises where sales are forging ahead fast *and* the company is loss-making, for instance when prices are cut to stimulate volume quickly in a new market. Both the rapidly mounting net current asset requirement and the loss-making have to be financed.

This is known at best as **"loss-leading"** and at worst as **"overtrading"**. Once a banker or investor senses this happening, he will quickly grow cautious about supporting the company further.

Banks will Suddenly Grow Cautious

Bankers *do* know about cash flow. They have to live with it on Friday, every Friday, in any number of companies up and down the country. Where there is insufficient cash to pay the wages, really agonising decisions result. Should the company be closed, with all the personal anguish it will cause, or should it be allowed to limp on, perhaps to face exactly the same agonising dilemma in as little as a week's time?

The apparently suprising scenarios set out at the start of Chapter II should now make better sense against this background.

Cash Loss *v* Stated Loss

As always, there is the need to distinguish between a stated loss, per the profit and loss account, and a cash loss. One company the author handled was running at an apparently frightening loss of £25,000 per month, but on closer examination there was not too much to worry about. It had a £30,000 monthly depreciation provision. It was in reality producing a cash-positive profit of £5,000 per month. It had *years* of life before it. This gave all the time needed to get the operation right.

Poor NCA Control

Conversely, a company that fails to control stocks and debtors properly suffers the same fate as the overtrading company, even where sales are not expanding materially. £1m turnover will require £270,000 NCA in a well controlled company. However if the NCA rate climbs to, say, 50% of turnover, £500,000 is suddenly needed. Again, immediate caution from the Bank Manager will result. He senses the lack of control.

P & L Plunge

Looking now at the detailed figurework given in Figure 19 and 20, we have already seen in Chapter V how this particular company that thought it was doing so well in nearly doubling sales and quadrupling order intake, was in fact heading straight for the ground in cash flow terms.

Cash Flow Plunge

Given the 27% of annual turnover rule, it is not difficult to appreciate what this does to working capital requirements (30/40) and cash flow (41/49). Stocks in Figure 19 (32/34) are 50% over budget, debtors (30/31) nearly double, unbudgeted fixed asset expenditure for plant, etc. (42) is needed to panic-handle the larger turnover. As a result of the plummeting gross margins (23) together with overheads 50% up (17), losses (45) also have to be financed. The "quick profit" calculations show this up clearly.

So the overdraft, instead of coming *down* by £13,000 (49) to £35,000 (56) goes up by £45,000 to £93,000 (£43,000 over the overdraft limit of £50,000), and creditors (39) almost double as the only means of taking up the excess. Net Creditor Strain goes out from £13,000, say 1½ weeks of purchases (5) at £30,000 per month, to £103,000, around 15 weeks above the 13-week norm.

Time Scale

All this can happen in just a few weeks. When an earlier draft of this book was being prepared an adverse swing of £90,000 in a single month seemed the top end of the scale for the rate at which things could go wrong in a company of the size illustrated. Not any more. A company with a turnover of £150,000 per month and profits of £15,000 has since produced an adverse swing of £200,000, in a single month, made up as follows:

Figure 22

	£'000
Increase NCA	80
Capital Expenditure	40
Dividend	20
Reduction in overdraft facilities	60
Total	200

It was first thought that the figure was spurious, that the calculation was somehow wrong. The company genuinely thought it was erroneous and decided to ignore the outcome. However, it wasn't wrong. After a certain amount of effort the company *were* convinced. All hell resulted, fortunately in time. Had extra strain on this scale remained undetected for more than a few weeks, severe, even fatal, damage could have resulted.

The extra reqirement in just one month "spent" the next 12 months pre-tax profits, the next 24 months post-tax profits, again illustrating the fundamental point that **profits are often quite insignificant in relation to the cash flow and funding need.**

Timetable to Armageddon

To control your business properly you *must*, therefore, have available the key information set out in Figures 19 and 20 within a very few days of the end of each month. The maximum period should not be more than fourteen days. If possible the figures should be on your desk within two to three. You then need to update the next few months budgets immediately the adverse trends begin to identify themselves. To the extent you cannot prevent the adverse trends happening, at least you will have produced an ever more accurate timetable to Armageddon.

Trends

Detecting the dynamic of a company involves detecting trends.

Figure 20 shows how, by building up the monthly actuals side by side, trends can start to be isolated. Sales (1) were £24,000 three months ago and order intake (25) £10,000. The following month, sales dropped to £20,000 and order intake remained stubbornly at £10,000. The company panicked, really slashed prices and were delighted to see sales more than double to £45,000 and order intake rocket to £80,000. However at what price (or rather lack of it) as has already been seen!

Raw material purchases (5) continue their relentless climb: £20,000, £30,000, £40,000. Labour (6) also: £4,000, £11,000, £15,000. Overheads (7): £8,000, £10,000, £12,000.

Margins plummet (12) (23): 42%, 20%, 11%.

Breakeven point rockets: £19,000, £50,000, £108,000. The gap between sales and breakeven opens from £5,000 favourable to £30,000 to £63,000 adverse, at a frightening rate. Losses mount: from £2,000 profit to £6,000 to £7,000 loss.

The Need for Quick Action to Reverse the Trends

The trends are speaking an all too clear message. Armageddon faces the company. **Management, by conscious action must now reverse these trends,** get overheads down, get gross margin percentages up and breakeven down, cut out raw material purchases, slim back again on labour, live on the fat contained in stocks and get stocks themselves down. There is a great deal that can be done in retargeting trends, drawing up a new business plan reflecting those trends and successfully "homing" the company into the new targets over a period of months.

Chapter IX

ENSURING A COMPANY IS ADEQUATELY FINANCED

Chapter VIII showed how a company's funding requirements can be narrowed down to just three aspects:

(1) Fixed Asset or "Capital" Expenditure for plant, buildings, vehicles etc.;
(2) Net Current Asset Requirement (e.g. 27% of turnover);
(3) "Intangibles" like losses, Research and Development Expenditure, etc:

Balance Sheet

The fact that these are the sole, prime capital needs of a company, tends to get obscured in conventional sets of accounts. Excellent books exist for the layman on the structure of Balance Sheets and how to find your way round them. There is a particularly good book available entitled "How to Understand and Use Company Accounts" by Mr. Roy Warren, a Partner of Robson Rhodes, Chartered Accountants. In order to keep everything as simple as possible, the form and layout of Balance Sheets will not therefore be discussed here.

Tangible Assets

Tangible *fixed* assets like plant and machinery and tangible *current* assets like stock and debtors, can be financed broadly by *loans*. Because of the security they offer, the assets can be taken and sold, "repossessed", if the loans are not repaid.

Caveats

However, there are at least four caveats:

(1) In the same way that a Building Society is unlikely to grant a 100% mortgage on your house, so lending against any asset is likely to be significantly less than its full value.
(2) A used asset will always have a lesser value than a new asset. Furthermore a special purpose asset, a particular type of electronic measuring instrument for instance, may only be of use for one particular company's operation and unsaleable eleswhere. Whatever

the cost the "realisable" value to the lender can be minimal and he will lend minimally against it. This may be particularly true of stocks and especially part-finished work like work-in-progress.

Debtors too may not have the full value ascribed to them. A customer sensing a company is in difficulties may raise all sorts of spurious "quality" or pricing complaints in order to delay payment or avoid it altogether. There may be genuine disputes. The product may not be what the customer ordered. The customer himself may be in financial difficulties.

For all these reasons, realisable value in a "forced sale" may be substantially less than book, or cost, value and accordingly can only be part-financed by loans.

(3) Even if the asset "cover" or security is adequate the loan has to be "serviced". Interest has to be paid regularly and the loan itself progressively repaid. If profitability and cash flow, on any rational basis, are inadequate to service interest and repayments for *all* the company's liabilities taken together, including hire purchase, factoring, leasing etc., the lender will see little prospect of getting his money back and will not lend.

(4) **"A lender prefers not to have more in a company than the owners themselves"**, at least until it is demonstrably successful, the so-called "One-to-One Gearing" concept, "1:1 loan/equity ratio."

"One-to-One Gearing"

The last feature is particularly important. If an owner invests £20,000 into a business by way of permanent capital, that is to say by way of "equity" a share investment that cannot be withdrawn, a bank will, in theory, provide up to another £20,000 as a secured loan. The bank may, however, be reluctant to provide more, at least in the first instance, because to do so would exceed the 1:1 loan/equity relationship. This is governed by the fact that **a bank's money is not its own to lend, but its depositors'; there must be a very high certainty of getting it back;** otherwise public confidence and the public deposit base, on which a bank's whole operation depends, could be withdrawn. . . .

If the company is profitable, profits retained in the company, after tax and dividends, will add to the shareholders stake of £20,000, enabling lending to be increased *pro rata* or perhaps by more than *pro rata* once success begins to be assured.

The Effect of Losses

Most companies make losses at one time or another, either on start-up or on hitting a bad trading patch. **Losses *reduce* the equity base and therefore the borrowing capacity.**

This may be particularly serious in the early years where it is unlikely there will be sufficient retained profits to absorb losses. Losses have to come instead out of shareholders' capital, again reducing borrowing capacity.

Negative Borrowing?

Suppose the owner has invested £20,000 in the company, which then makes a £25,000 loss. The £20,000 *positive* equity stake becomes £5,000 *negative*. If a further loss of, say, £25,000 follows, the net equity base of the company becomes £30,000 *negative*. In theory the bank will lend *minus* £30,000 in such circumstances. In practice they will put the company under strong pressure to repay even the basic £20,000, let alone agree to lend more, and may anyway call for additional personal security. The *company* has no security to offer.

Unless the borrowing base can be restored, the company is in very serious trouble, particularly when the NCA requirement associated with building up turnover fast to get past breakeven point is added. It can only be done by injecting additional outside equity.

The following table illustrates the point:

Figure 23

Stage	(1)	(2)	(3)	(4)
Owners Share Capital	20	20	20	20
Outside Share Capital	—	—	80	80
Retained Profits (Losses)	—	(50)	(50)	100
Total Equity	20	(30)	50	200
Borrowings	20	?	30	300
Total Funding	40	NEG	80	500
Gearing (Borrowing : Equity)	1:1	NEG	0·6:1	1·5:1

Outside Investor Stays in a Minority

It might be assumed that as the outside equity stake in this example is *four times* the owner's own equity stake, the original owner will be left with only 20% of his company. While this might have been true in the past, a number of venture and development capital funds have been set up in the last few years, like indeed the Fund the author presently manages, **to provide the amount required and yet stay strictly in a minority.**

Separate Class of Shares

It is done by putting in the investment as a separate class of shares with reduced capital and voting rights, say 30% (in return, say, for enhanced income rights). The picture will then look as follows:

Figure 24

	£'000	%
Owner—Ordinary Shares	20	70%
Outside Investor—Preference Shares	80	30%
Total Equity	100	100%

Such a move will also enhance the borrowing capacity of the company up to fourfold.

Gearing-up—Two Aspects

There are two aspects of gearing up:

(1) **Gearing-up the Owner's equity base in the company** (by a factor of 4 in this case);
(2) **Gearing-up the Borrowing** (assume for illustrative purposes also by a factor of 4).

Theoretical Benefit

This can change the picture dramatically, as follows:

Figure 25

	Before £'000	After £'000
First Stage Gearing		
Owner	20	20
Outside Investor	—	80
Total Equity	20	100
Second Stage Gearing		
Borrowings	20	100
Total Funding	40	200

Practical Outcome
In practice a bank will not, at least in the first instance, go as far as full 1:1 loan/equity gearing, particularly if losses are in prospect. The "gearing" will be assessed as if those losses had already happened and a picture nearer Stage (3) of Figure 23 will result in practice.

However, as the company comes into cumulative profit, lending can forge ahead, perhaps going well beyond the equity base, Stage (4).

Dynamic Representation
A graphic "dynamic" representation of this run-in cycle, common to nearly all start-ups and young companies, is illustrated in Figure 28 on page 80. Somewhat appropriately, it is known as the "death valley" curve.

Company Failure Rates
According to a study taken from VAT returns, 50% of companies set-up in the UK since 1975 have subsequently disappeared. What proportion were lost through the various factors of amalgamation, reconstruction or outright failure is not known. However, the death rate in the last category is very high, particularly in the first 2 or 3 years of a company's life. Undercapitalisation combined with insufficient understanding, by management and owners alike, of basic cash flow issues, basic cash flow needs and the problems associated with those needs, are the overwhelming factors, in both senses of the word.

Large Companies don't Trade at First with Smaller
Incidentally, a major company is unlikely to trade with a new company, however good its products or services, for at least 3 years, for this very reason. Be warned in advance! Your product may effectively be plugging the major company's production lines into your own and they just dare not risk being let down (see Chapter XIV).

Similar Gearing Problems Occur in Established Companies
Existing well established companies can just as much find themselves in the same position after a bout of loss-making, heavy capital expenditure on plant and equipment, new product and market development or rapid escalation in turnover as orders and sales forge ahead. The same solutions need to be applied. The Balance Sheet must first be strengthened with an equity injection to re-create the borrowing power needed to finance the expansion.

Figure 26

£100K EQUITY INJECTION—REQUIREMENTS

	Before £'000	After £'000	Need £'000	Funded £'000
Fixed Assets	100	100		
Less: Hire Purchase	(30)	(30)		
NFA	70	70		
Intangibles—R & D etc	40	40		
Stock + Debtors	290	290		
Less Creditors	(180)	(110)	+ 70	
NCA	110	180		
Less Bank O/D (Limit 100)	(120)	(90)	+ 30	
	(10)	90		
Net Assets	100*	200*	100	
Deduct: Intangibles	(40)	(40)		
"Net Capital Resources"	60**	160**		

FUNDED

	Before	After	Need	Funded
Equity—Owner	30	30		
Outside Investor(s)	—	100***		+ 100
	30	130		
Retained Profits (Losses)	70	70		
Total Net Assets as above	100	200		+ 100
"Off Balance Sheet"—Leasing	30	30		

Equity Uplift	NIL	× 3⅓***
Capital Gearing:		
Apparent Loan/Equity Ratio	150/100*	120/200*
	1.5/1.0	0.6/1.0
Real Gearing Ratio	180/60**	150/160**
	3.0/1.0	0.9/1.0
Target Under	1.0 /1.0	1.0 /1.0

Now that the 79/82 recession is easing (at long last) an increasing number of companies will find themselves in this position. "Cash flow goes out of the window as companies expand." To avoid such dangers, which are bound to rear their head at *the* most inconvenient moment, say during a crucial market expansion, the problems need to be identified well in advance and dealt with effectively, well in advance.

Measuring Actual Gearing Ratio

You can measure whether the equity base in your own company is adequate by reference to Figure 26, which shows how you can calculate your own actual gearing ratio. You should do this regularly, and do it well ahead from the forward budget, to avoid any danger of "under capitalisation" building up.

Apparent Gearing Ratio

The simple version of the loan/equity ratio is calculated under the first column. Loans total £150,000 (£30,000 hire purchase + £120,000 bank overdraft). Equity totals £100,000 (owner's shares £30,000, + retained profits £70,000). This gives an *apparent* gearing ratio of 150/100 or 1.5 to 1.

Bankers Gearing Ratio

Because banks are worried about the cash flow of a company and about its ability to service and repay loans they may take a stricter view. This consists of adding factors like leasing to the borrowings side, £30,000 in this case, taking total borrowings to £180,000. They may also deduct intangible assets from the asset side, reducing notional equity to that represented by the tangible assets only. In this case net assets are reduced by £40,000 to £60,000, to arrive at what a bank will call the Company's "Net Capital Resources".

Combine the two factors as shown and the banker's real gearing ratio becomes 180/60 or 3.0 to 1.0, which will lead him to regard the company as being in a severely overstretched position.

Your Borrowing Problem

Whatever your own thoughts on the subject that is the way he will view it, whatever the merits of your company, whatever the size of the order book, whatever the prospect of sparkling growth, worsening gearing can be a veritable time bomb ticking away inside a company, getting ever more dangerous as sales and orders build up and the NCA requirement moves further and further ahead of profit contribution. It is likely to explode at the worst possible moment, when the bank eventually *has* to call a halt.

The Solution

There are three ways out:

(1) Improve profitability, keeping turnover down to keep the NCA requirements down, which of course is the dominant source of the funding need, and gradually build up the necessary equity base from *after-tax* profit retention. It could be a long haul, measurable in years rather than months.

(2) Slash turnover to reduce the NCA requirement whilst at least maintaining *some* profitability.

(3) Inject more equity. An extra £100,000 would restore full borrowing capacity to the company, second column, allowing rapid, profitable growth to take place. There are a number of funds providing such capital including, of course, the fund run by the author.

The Management Buy-Out (Figure 27)

Another case where an injection of outside equity can be valuable is to facilitate the "management buyout". Mr. X is a bright, resourceful, executive who wants to do his own thing. He identifies a company for sale for, say, £250,000 (first column of Figure 27) asks his accountant to value the assets, second column, and decides to go ahead.

However he can find only £50,000 of his own and friends' money to put into the company and needs help with the rest.

If he tries to raise the balance of £200,000 all by borrowing, column (1), even if successful, the loans will swamp the borrowing capacity of the company and severely endanger the ongoing operation, which is reflected in the adverse gearing of infinity! Intangibles of £90,000 and loans of £200,000 have been deducted from net assets of £250,000 leaving net capital resources of *minus* £40,000. The company simply will not be able to borrow as it expands. Indeed after a few months the lenders may well exert pressure to *reduce* the facilities.

If the company is going to be lossmaking for a period after the buyout, which it may well be while the new team is bedding down the operation, the extra money should be raised wholly as equity, column (2). Alternatively a loan/equity mixture might be appropriate, column (3). Here again development capital organisations like the author's would come into the picture, attaching, say, 30% capital rights to their £175,000 stake, leaving the new owner with 70% for his £50,000.

Figure 27

MANAGEMENT BUY-OUT
REQUIREMENT

	Company being sold £'000	"Assets being Acquired" £'000
Fixed Assets	100	130
H.P.	(30)	(30)
	70	100
R&D/Goodwill*	40	90*
Stocks + Debtors—Creditors	180	150
Bank Overdraft	(90)	(90)
Net Assets	200	250
Purchase Price	250	
Goodwill, thus	50*	

FUNDED

	(1) All loan	(2) All Equity	(3) Loan/Equity
Equity: Owner(s)	50	50	50
Outside Investor(s)	—	200	175
	50	250	225
Bank/Investor Loans	200	—	25
Total as above	250	250	250
Apparent Gearing	320/50 6.4/1.0	120/250 0.5/1.0	145/225 0.6/1.0
Real Gearing	320/(40) Infinity	120/160 0.8/1.0	145/135 1.1/1.0

Figure 28

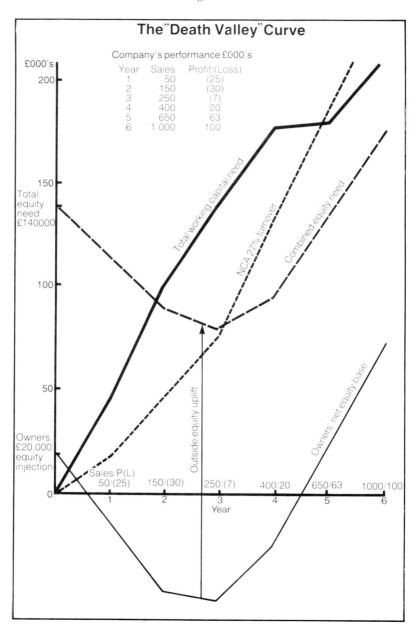

Share Purchase (Figure 29)

Another version of the same process is where just one shareholder, perhaps a controlling shareholder, wants to retire and sell out for say £170,000. Perhaps his son wants to come in, or a well qualified executive from big business who wants to do "his own thing", but can afford only £30,000. A development capital organisation like the author's would provide the rest.

Figure 29

SOLUTION

Outside Investor pays Mr. X £140,000, and converts the shares to reduced-voting Preference Shares, thus enhancing stake of Mr. Y and, if desired, the ongoing stake of existing shareholder(s) Messrs. Z.

	Before		After	
	£'000	%	£'000	%
Mr. X	170	85%	—	—
Mr. Y	—	—	30	35%
Messrs. Z	30	15%	30	35%
	200	100%	60	70%
Outside Investor	—	—	140	30%
	200	100%	200	100%

Chapter X

BUSINESS PLAN — FOR A SERVICE COMPANY

The Cash Flow formats given in the Appendix are set out in sufficient detail to cope with the more complicated type of manufacturing company. Service companies are simpler. For the most part they are selling skilled hours directly and therefore have little or no *stock* requirement. A business where the services are sold principally for cash will also only have a small *debtor* requirement.

Structuring a Business Plan for a New Operation

Let's now use the example of a service company to PLAN a business, to see if it is intrinsically viable; and if not—and most companies are not at first attempt—to decide what has to be done to *make* it viable.

A Cookery Course

Imagine for a moment you are an investor and a very pretty girl in her 30s comes in with a beautiful face, lovely figure—and two large . . . cookery books under her arm. She asks for financial support for her project. The cash flow formats at Appendix will deal with the most complex type of company, like a multi-national. Let's now go to the extreme other end of the scale and see what happens when they are used to plan an operation as simple as a cookery course.

Basic Viability must be Checked

You do your potential customer no service if you are lulled and seduced by her charms and go ahead regardless without checking the essential viability of her operation. She will lose her money. You will lose yours. Perhaps more important she will lose face, self-esteem, self-respect and the respect of others if the operation does not work. She will blame you, however irrationally.

You owe her a duty, for her sake, for the sake of the people she is going to employ, her clients, her suppliers, to use your skills to ensure she is not allowed to go ahead until all the elements you know are required to make a business work *are* in place. You cannot guarantee to suceed of course. Business in the last resort is subject to all the vagaries of the market place over which no-one has control, but at least with careful planning the odds can be shortened.

Key Considerations

Where do you start? Firstly the cash flow has to be sufficient to cover *all* costs, such as any overheads between courses, advertising costs and so on despite the impossibility of knowing for certain in advance what numbers the course will attract. (We can successfully steer round this apparently intractable problem as we shall see, which involves pitching the breakeven point in the right place.) Secondly, the funding itself must be correctly structured. Service companies usually have few assets to support borrowing. Other methods must be found.

Specific Case History

It is intended to run 4 basic skills courses of 5 weeks each; 3 special occasion courses of 5 weeks each; 1 French cooking course of 5 weeks (to be conducted by the sponsor herself); 2 family meal courses of 5 weeks each; and 2 Christmas Special courses of 5 weeks each; making 12 courses in all.

This can be programmed as either 6 courses running simultaneously for 10 weeks, or 3 for 20, or 2 for 30, or 1 for 60.

Getting the Time Scales Right

Clearly the 60 week option is out, as it exceeds a full year. Holidays and 'dead' periods around Christmas, Easter and the Summer holidays also need to be allowed for. Given that fixed costs accrue with time, the longer the time scale the higher the costs that have to be recouped out of each course and the more that will need to be charged.

The alternatives are, provisionally, to run 2 "terms" a year of 20 weeks each, with 3 courses running simultaneously, or 3 "terms" a year of 10 weeks, with 6 courses running simultaneously. The latter will be the lowest intrinsic cost version and therefore the lowest priced, but can sufficient numbers be attracted, which parallels the volume v price problem from the Mini onwards?

Cost Side

Suspending judgement for the moment, let's try to assess likely costs and put them into some kind of fixed and variable groupings:

(1) There will be the cost of food, say £10 per course per pupil. Here we have a genuine variable cost. No pupil, no food.

(2) One person is needed to run each course, say £50 per week per course.

(3) Rent of premises. Premises can be hired for £60 per week, sufficient to take 6 courses simultanously of up to 10 people each.

(4) Sundry costs, typing, postage, travel and insurance amount to, say, £12 per week.

(5) Fuel, heating and lighting are likely to cost £5 per course per week.
(6) Finally, there is advertising. At least £600 will be spent to attract sufficient custom per term.
(7) £100 worth of kitchen equipment will also be needed.

Income

It is intended to charge £50 per pupil per 5 week course. Payment will be required 3 weeks after a course finishes, soft terms designed to help attract the necessary custom. (In practice no sponsor would be so unwise as to suggest payment *after* rather than *before* the event. But it helps to illustrate an important principle of cash flow, as we shall see.)

Question, will it work?

You might like to work out the issues for yourself before reading on.
Solution Allocate fixed costs as follows:

Figure 30

COSTS PER TERM

	6 courses at a time over 10 weeks £	3 courses at a time over 20 weeks £
Staff	3,000	3,000
Rent	600	1,200
Sundry	120	240
Heating and Lighting	300	Say 400
Advertising	600	600
Start-up Costs (ignored for simplicity)	—	—
Total	4,620	5,440
Total Costs per course	£385	£455

This must be compared with "sales" income of £50 course. Deduct £10 for food. Gross margin is £40 course. So far so good. No assumptions have yet had to be made.

Break even is Where?

Now for the critical next step. Divide total costs per course by the unit gross margin of £40 to determine **number of pupils per course needed to break even**:

Figure 31a

Breakeven No. per Course	10	12

Non-Starter

The premises only holds 10 people per course! So this represents 100% and 120% of capacity respectively, just to breakeven. It also implies the need to attract a *minimum* of 120 people per 10 week term or 144 people per 20 week term.

Scope for Raising Prices? Reducing Costs?

What would happen if prices were raised to £60 gross, £50 net, per course and if advertising were cut by, say, £200 per term to reflect the lower volumes now going to be needed?

Cost would come down marginally to £370 and £440 per course.

New Level of Breakeven

Breakeven point would now be 7 and 9. Still very high. Let's raise prices to £65 gross, £55 net, and try to negotiate a better deal on the rent, saving, say, £100. By scheduling courses to overlap to some extent can we save, say, ⅙ of the biggest item of cost, labour, by employing only 5 instead of 6 instructors?

If so Rework Viability

Costs are now as shown in Figure 32. The operation is now beginning to have the right "feel" about it and one can start planning the Profit and Loss Account and cash flow sides.

Importance of Management Knowledge

A particularly striking aspect of physically having to go through the procedure just mentioned is that it brings home to management just how important it is going to be to keep costs ruthlessly pegged to the levels now arrived at, which self-evidently is not going to be easy, with the need to react *immediately* if future unavoidable increases occur.

Figure 32

COSTS PER TERM

	6 courses at a time over 10 weeks	3 courses at a time over 20 weeks
	£	£
Staff	2,500	2,500
Rent	500	1,000
Sundry	120	240
Heating and lighting	300	400
Advertising	400	400
	3,820	4,540
Costs per 5 week course	£318	£378
Unit income	£55	£55
Breakeven No.	6	7

Need for MD Himself to Draw Up the Plan

It should really be for the Managing Director himself or herself to plan the business in this way in the first instance. An accountant or other adviser should not be asked to do it for him. Why? **The MD needs to experience in a very direct and personal way just what does happen if the various parameters are not structured in the way they *must* be to achieve viability. The dividing line between success and failure can be wafer thin, as will be appreciated from the example just given, which is typical of many, if not most, companies.** The MD who subsequently puts that plan into effect thus needs to carry in his or her mind's eye the harsh lessons of what must be done to meet that plan when actually running the company. "Much better to go bust on paper than go bust in practice".

Market Survey

The final decision now to be taken is to make a guess, but **an informed guess, the first one we have made**, of how many people a 5 week course might attract at a price of £65. Not until now have we had to introduce *any* assumptions into the calculations. A rigorous market survey would be done. **But it must only be done at this stage once all the "bench-marks" needed for viability have been worked out and are, therefore, fully known about. Otherwise the survey, conducted for the arbitrarily chosen initial sales** price of, say, £50 rather than the needed price of £65, **will be worthless. The same is true for any market survey for any company.**

If response is a bit lukewarm, it might be better to run 3 simultaneous courses every 5 weeks for 20 weeks twice a year, than 6 courses over 20 weeks three times, even though the intrinsic profitability of the latter is a little better, breaking even at 6 rather than 7 people per course and generating 3 term's income per year instead of 2. The safer route would be to go for the lower level operation, at least initially until actual market experience has built up. Having made this decision, let's guess, from firm market intelligence, that the courses will attract on average 8 people each at £65 per 5 week course.

Actual P&L Plan

The definition of "sales" is not when the money is received but when the work is done. As will be seen from Figure 33 the Profit and Loss Account

Figure 33

3 SIMULTANEOUS COURSES OVER FOUR 5 WEEK PERIODS

Income—First Term

Month	Jan.	Feb.	Mar.	Apr.	May	June
	£	£	£	£	£	£
Sales (3 × 8 people paying £65 per month)	Nil	Nil	1,560	1,560	1,560	1,560
Cost of food 3 × 8 × £10	Nil	Nil	240	240	240	240
Gross Margin	Nil	Nil	1,320	1,320	1,320	1,320

	Costs					
	Training		Operational			
Staff	300	300	625	625	625	625
Rent	250	250	250	250	250	250
Sundry	100	100	60	60	60	60
Heating and Lighting	25	50	100	100	100	100
Advertising	200	200	—	—	—	—
Total Fixed Costs	875	900	1,035	1,035	1,035	1,035
Pre Tax Profit/(Loss)	(875)	(900)	285	285	285	285

has been planned into two 4 month courses separated by 2 month gaps, allowing at the start for one or two months to get going and avoiding holidays, assuming for simplicity 1 month = 5 weeks.

"Sensitivity" factors

Every extra person earns another £55 profit per 5 week course. A loss or gain of one person per course on all 12 courses reduces or increases profits by £660. Maximum profit is therefore £2,060 at full capacity.

The company breaks even at just under 7 people per course, loses £580 at 6 per course, loses £1,240 at 5 per course, and so on. **The breakeven point is only *just* in the right place, which places additional emphasis on ensuring the market survey is properly done and that cost targets are ruthlessly met, or bettered, in actual operation.**

Figure 34

Check

			£
Prediction	A 5 week course earns 8 × £55	=	440
	Costs (Figure 32)		378
	Profit per course		62
	Number of courses		12
	Overall Profit		744
Compare	4 weeks profit at £285 (Figure 33)	=	1,140
	Less advertising (charged in earlier months)		400
	Net Profit		740
			O.K.

Overdraft requirements

The cash flow works out as shown in figure 35. The closing overdraft reflects the fact that the run-in costs, principally training ("intangibles"), exceed the first term's profits by £635 (Figure 33), and £100 of capital expenditure also has to be funded. At this stage the Profit and Loss Account should also be reworked to include interest on the closing overdrafts at, say, 1% per month.

Cash Flow

Figure 35

Month	Jan.	Feb.	Mar.	Apr.	May	June	July
	£	£	£	£	£	£	£
Debtors	—	—	1,560	1,560	1,560	1,560	—
Stock (say)	—	200	250	250	250	250	—
	—	200	1,810	1,810	1,810	1,810	—
Creditors (say)	—	(100)	(250)	(250)	(250)	(250)	—
Net Current Assets	—	100	1,560	1,560	1,560	1,560	—
+/(−) **NCA**	—	100	1,460	—	—	—	(1,560)
Capital Expenditure	100	—	—	—	—	—	—
(Profit)/Losses	875	900	(285)	(285)	(285)	(285)	—
Net Cash (In)/Out	975	1,000	1,175	(285)	(285)	(285)	(1,560)
Closing Overdraft	975	1,975	3,150	2,865	2,580	2,295	735

What if no overdraft is available?

Suppose, however, the sponsor cannot raise the security necessary to support such an overdraft. The pupils are due to pay 3 weeks after the course's end. Pupils might never be heard of again, rendering what they owe uncollectable. Or they may dispute the value of what they have been taught and refuse to pay. There is no security in the "debtors", therefore, for the bank. Even with the £250 of food stock, it is likely to deteriorate so rapidly and be so capable of pilferage that there is no comfort here either. The only other security on offer is £100 worth of kitchen equipment which is, of course, minimal. Finally the sponsor may not want, or be able, to guarantee the overdraft from her own personal resources.

Change payment terms

Because of the bad debt problem alone, it would be highly advisable to make payment on registration a condition of enrolling for the course. This would not only dramatically improve cash flow but would firm-up the "will" of those attending. Having paid, they are likely to see it through. If the cost is going to deter them, it is as well to know about it in advance, before costs are incurred on the courses themselves.

Reworked Cash Flow

The cash flow would then become:

Figure 36

Month	Jan.	Feb.	Mar.	Apr.	May.	June	July
	£	£	£	£	£	£	£
Debtors	—	—	—	—	—	—	—
Stock	—	200	250	250	250	250	—
(Payments in advance)	—	(6,240)	(4,680)	(3,120)	(1,560)	—	—
	—	(6,040)	(4,430)	(2,870)	(1,310)	250	—
Creditors	—	(100)	(250)	(250)	(250)	(250)	—
Net Current Assets	—	(6,140)	(4,680)	(3,120)	(1,560)	—	—
+/(−) NCA	—	(6,140)	1,460	1,560	1,560	1,560	—
Capital Expenditure	100	—	—	—	—	—	—
(Profit)/Loss	875	900	(285)	(285)	(285)	(285)	—
Net Cash (In)/Out	975	(5,240)	1,375	1,275	1,275	1,275	—
Closing Cash Balance	—	4,265	3,090	1,815	540	---	—
Closing Overdraft	975	—	—	—	—	735	735

The overdraft at the end of the day of course ends up the same as before. *Some* facility, say £1,000, is thus needed, but the bank is in credit most of the time.

Lack of Borrowing Power

Most service companies suffer this lack of borrowing power because of the comparative absence of stocks and debtors, a point that needs watching in structuring payment terms and funding.

Other Service Companies

The Cookery Course just quoted has a particularly good gross margin of 85%. Most service or distribution companies operate at the other end of the scale on very fine margins. When Sainsbury's announced its results for 1982, much play was made of the fact that gross margin (after food, staff and transport costs, the latter being a significant item for a supermarket) had increased from 4.0% the previous year to 4.4%. A 0.4% improvement may not sound so impressive until it is realised that it represents a massive 10% increase in real income, on £2–3bn of turnover.

Fractional losses or gains in gross margin percentage can make all the difference between success and failure for service operations. Gross margin should, therefore, be very precisely measured each month (or week) to the nearest one, or even two, places of decimals. Even very small departures, good or bad, should be relentlessly hunted down and identified.

Why can Service and Distribution Companies Operate at such Low Margins?

Very low margins imply very high breakeven. Very high breakeven implies very high working capital requirements . . . so very special measures need to be taken to reduce the requirement.

A supermarket succeeds to the extent that it can:
 (1) Sell for cash. There are, therefore, no debtors.
 (2) Limit stock, of necessity anyway with perishable food items, to no more than a few days, which calls for super-efficient supply lines and exceptional planning and administration procedures extending months, perhaps even years, into the future.
 (3) Get good credit terms from suppliers, certainly getting one-month terms and if possible two to three.

Positive NCA Figure

Given sufficient ingenuity, cash can be generated "up-front". Instead of forming a cash *need*, the NCA figure can produce a cash *surplus*. This cash can be invested, often on a substantial scale, to produce interest income, which will often rival the scale of the trading profits themselves . . . which in turn permits the company to operate on still lower gross margins.

Another Example

An intermediary operation might be a beer, wines and spirits wholesaling company running at gross margins of between 8% and 12%. Inevitably the market is extremely price-sensitive with standard, established products of this nature. Volume is needed to compensate in profit terms for the poor margins, but fractional increases in price beyond what is acceptable in the market place will drive away business on a large scale.

Reliability of Supply

The company has to have something to offer for which it can charge a small premium, like total reliability of supply on a "same-day" basis. The retailer can then carry lower stocks, easing *his* funding and interest problem and he should, therefore, be prepared to pay a little more. As we have seen, it may be "little" to him, a percentage point or two, but it can mean a great deal for the company, in both senses.

Tight deal with Suppliers

Similarly because of the low margins, a service or distribution company needs to be able to do a very "tight" deal with its suppliers, striking a fine balance between getting the good credit terms it needs to fund the operation and making a hard bargain on price to create adequate margins.

Tight deal with Customers

Even so the company will need to be ruthless with its own financial control and organisation, not offering the customer credit terms, or only offering them against payment within 2–3 weeks at most, and carrying minimal stocks consistent with being able to give the customer the service he needs.

Chapter XI

DOVETAILING YOUR BUSINESS TO THE MARKET

Having established an accurate means of monitoring cash flow we come back to the main thrill, drama and fascination of business—accurate dovetailing of your product or service to the market place.

By How Much does Sales Volume Change with Changes in Sales Price?

You need for a start to find out how price-sensitive your product is, at least in its existing form.

Going Up

What does happen to volume when you raise prices by 10%? By 20%? By 50%? You should be able to find out by good market research and by marketing trial and error, selecting versions of the product to sell into one-off outlets in a way that will not upset your main customer base or regular line of business.

Going Down

Conversely, what does happen when you reduce prices?

How "Strong" is your Product's Price in the Market-Place?

Armed with this information you will know how durable your product is, how much your customer wants it for its unique qualities; or whether for example, it has few special features and simply sells on price.

Yet another aspect of the Mini story is illustrative. BMC had a unique product, opening up whole new market areas like the second-car family, yet it was priced sufficiently low to be "competitive" with the Ford Popular. It had so many novel features to induce the customer to buy that the attraction of cheapness didn't need to be offered as well. Indeed a premium, a "uniqueness", a "rarity", a "quality" price might have further added to its attraction. But it was down-priced and it helped to bring a fine organisation to its knees. Kenwood had a better food mixer than anyone else. The company didn't need to price so "competitively". But at one stage its prices *were* marked down unduly. As as a direct result Kenwood in the mid 60's got into acute trouble too. There are many, many other examples from the history of the UK industrial scene over the years.

When you do this exercise for your own company you may find an unexpected result. Occasionally an increase in price will actually increase volume! There can be two reasons.

Quality—Convenience

Cheapness is often associated, however wrongly, with poor quality in the mind of the customer, deterring him from buying. Just before the last War a way was discovered of turning waste coal dust into a useful product by compressing it into oval brickettes. This made it not only indistinguishable from coal in burning qualities, but it was easier for the housewife to handle.

Because the product used waste dust and the process itself was cheap, the inventor found he could put it on the market at substantially less than the normal price of coal and still make a very acceptable margin. He thought he was on to a winner. But of course it failed miserably. Sales stubbornly refused to take off and within 18 months the venture was virtually bankrupt.

In desperation he turned to an experienced business friend who told him at once what was wrong. No-one believed genuine coal could be sold at so low a price. Because of the convenience of use he had to price it *above* the price of coal (regardless of how much he would then be making; that was his perk for the ingenuity of the idea). With great reluctance he did so . . . and Coalite never looked back.

Quality—Reliability

The second aspect, in a sense, has to do with quality too. Many products are not sold to an end user, but go into equipment made by another company (an Original Equipment Manufacturer or OEM). Like you, their viability also depends on reliability, in two senses:

(1) the need to achieve uninterrupted production flow, as discussed in Chapter XIV;

(2) the need to win and keep customer satisfaction.

An experienced business buying from another will intuitively know how much it costs to build quality and reliability into a product. If the price is too low the potential customer will deduce either:

(3) quality has *not* been built in; or

(4) it has been built in, but at a cost that risks sooner or later ruining the company. At the very least, it may so weaken the operation, by progressively starving it of the funds that it needs to plough back into R&D, etc., that it will fall behind in the market place. Your

customer's *own* future may crucially depend on you being able to keep up to date with new product generation, to enable *him* to keep ahead of the competition.

So the larger company, sensing this lack of business "bite", will be wary of placing large orders, or even many orders at all.

However, as soon as prices are put up to the "right" level, it creates the feeling of:

(1) a more confident and tough-minded management team, with an attitude that is likely to spin off into other areas of the business, good styling, innovative products, reliability of delivery, etc.;

(2) built-in quality that *can* be afforded, to the present and future benefit of the customer.

An Example

Take the real-life case of a company making electronic units for computers and word processors. It had a healthy order book (four months' work) and felt it could safely increase prices by 20%–25%. If it slowed the build-up of orders, all well and good, in making the production problem more manageable.

In fact orders increased by a further 80% within 5 weeks of the rise for just the reason given!

As a very rough rule of thumb you are under-pricing if you are not losing around, say, 30% of the orders you would otherwise be getting, on price grounds alone.

Price-Cutting Competition

When a competitor comes into your market with vastly lower prices, don't follow him down. He is probably desperate to buy volume at any price (literally). The solution is to let him have it, for the very reasons explained earlier. It is the quickest way of weakening his operation or maybe even forcing him out of business altogether. This removes a competitor from the field and it is exactly the sort of business you *want* to place his way, particularly in *quantity!*

It is quite different when a genuine competitor emerges on the scene with a genuinely cheaper and better product because it has been designed that way to achieve lower cost whilst still giving a very respectable margin. You do, then, have to re-design your own range very quickly in order to maintain gross margin so you can compete, in the way explained, for instance, in Chapter XV.

The Same Basic Economic Rules apply to Everyone

But remember the same economic rules apply to everyone, even foreign competition. Anything they can do you can do given sufficient ingenuity. One of the main differences between the British and, for instance, the Japanese lies in the fact that the latter as a race seem to understand the issues set out in this book rather better and are able to act accordingly, succeeding thereby in building a greater number of really durable businesses. In Japan these things *are* much more widely and more fully understood, by scientists, by research engineers, by academics, by salesmen, by accountants and right down the line from the boardroom both inside and outside business.

Japanese and Far East Competition

When Japanese efforts are examined against the altogether more exacting perceptions and standards set out in this book, they are often found not to be so frighteningly invincible. A leading UK electronics company recently researched into just why certain Japanese products were so competitive with their own. To their surprise, they found the material content in their own product was substantially less, being only 70% of the Japanese figure. The UK company, too, were more highly automated and rates of pay were certainly no higher.

Business Understanding by Engineers

What had gone wrong? One suspects the UK company was over-automated. Simpler production methods might have resulted in a lower breakeven point. Overheads were loaded up in installing sophisticated, capital-intensive equipment. The effect of the higher overhead may inadvertently have come to outweigh the benefits achieved from lower material and labour usage per unit, and therefore from improved gross margins. The formula given in Figure 3, on Page 19, determines the issues.

The engineers who designed the UK line, by their professional training and outlook, are unlikely to have been taught how best to think about business issues in the way envisaged in this book. So it is unlikely they would have designed the product itself and the production line in general whilst keeping the need, for instance, to optimise breakeven point uppermost in mind.

They were asked to design a "labour-saving, high volume line" on the unspoken assumption that this was *bound* to minimise costs and so bound to maximise the chances of being able to compete successfully in the market place, as if price were the only factor.

We have now seen how harmful this one-sided view can be. The dynamic of the volume side, on costs, on prices, also needs to be taken into account. A product is not going to have to sell just on price alone, but in the volume a sophisticated production line demands. There may be less to be gained from inherent price advantage than lost in the disadvantage of having to force high volume onto an unsuspecting market place in order to keep the lines full, which the market may be too small to absorb anyway, so leading to undue pricing cutting...

Another Case History

In January 1982 the author was called down to a company in the light engineering industry that had been in existence for twelve years. The MD, a very experienced engineer in his 50s, was on the point of giving up and selling his assets to the company next door (painful). Sales of the main product had declined over the past year, hit by the recession. Turnover was so low at £10,000 per month that even after cutting overheads right back to give a much improved monthly breakeven point of £21,200, the gap was still too large to be closed. As the last straw the order book, which had previously stood at £40,000, was suddenly decimated when a big customer cancelled £30,000 worth, perhaps suspecting the plight the company was in and himself suffering from the recession.

The MD was asked what his gross margin was?

"5% to 7%", he said.

"Really?" we said. "We knew you were in trouble, but we had not realised it was quite on the scale a 5% to 7% gross margin would imply!"

He, like so many in similar circumstances, seemed thrown by the question.

Net Margin

He was of course talking about *net* margin, net profit after deducting all costs, including overheads. Gross margin as a concept seemed new to him. This meant, of course, he was unlikely to have a sufficient perception of the difference between fixed and variable costs to be able to make the right decisions in running the busness. For instance, it was unlikely he would be costing and pricing his products correctly, particularly in the sharply changed recessionary conditions of the time.

Reliance on Accountant

Like any experienced "product" man, the MD naturally turned to his accountant for advice and guidance on all financial matters in his business.

His accountant was a very able partner in a highly-regarded local firm of auditors. Each month the two sat down round a table and ran the business between them.

Introduction of Conventional Costing System

The accountant many years before had introduced the company to a wholly orthodox, conventional costing system, which was then, and still is, in widespread use throughout British industry.

Under this system, briefly, products are priced at material cost plus a multiple of labour cost, say 3½ times labour cost. This is a reflection of the need to "recover" overheads and allow some margin for profit, which the 2½ times mark-up is designed to achieve.

Effects

Although not apparent to the uninitiated, the effect of this treatment is to spread overheads over a fixed, very specific, volume of output, probably set many years before in better days and unlikely to have been kept fully up to date since.

Costings will therefore be correct at one precise (unmeasured) volume and wrong at all other volumes. The greater the difference, the worse the error.

Lower Sales Volume

At all lower volumes the company will be under-costing and therefore under-pricing its products. Such a company will get into undue trouble in a recession, as indeed happened to an unwarrantably large number of British companies between 1979 and 1982.

High Sales Volumes

Conversely, when market opportunities do occur and there is scope for increased volume at the right price, the system will over-cost and over-price, leading perhaps to valuable market opportunities being lost.

"Norm" Volume

The system is only correct for the one very specific volume of output inherent in its calculation. It is thus only suitable for a steady-state company operating in a steady-state, fixed volume, market.

Static Concept

A static market. It's a static concept! What is needed is a dynamic concept, a method to allow a company to price accurately at a moment's notice over all ranges of volume and price, just as a barrow-boy prices in "trading" successfully in the market place.

Let's see how the new concept can be made to work by returning to two very worried men, the engineer at one end of the table and the accountant at the other, both, after 3 years of recession, at an uttter loss to know what to do.

Standard Remedies had been tried

The conventional wisdom, if not selling enough, is to drop prices and try and sell more. That had indeed been tried, but it only seemed to lead to still greater losses (for reasons that should by now be fully clear to the reader).

Overheads had been pared to the bone. There seemed nowhere else to go but to shut up shop. A familiar enough story isn't it in countless thousands of light-engineering companies up and down the country, in the Midlands in particular?

There is, however, a very clear way forward, which may at first sight seem utterly daft and to fly in the face of all commonsense and convention. It is likely to result in two men in white coats waiting for you as you leave the building if you fail to get your message across properly . . .

Getting a Grip on Sales Prices

The MD was asked, admittedly somewhat tongue-in-cheek, what would happen if he doubled his prices?

"I would go bust", he said.

"You are going bust already" we said. "Would you be any worse off?"

"Of course" he said "I would lose three quarters of even my existing volume of business".

"Would that matter?" we said.

"Of course it would. I would go bust."

Sensing we had been here before we said,

"But would you?"

Little exercise:

Figure 37

EFFECT ON GROSS MARGIN OF DOUBLING PRICES AND IN CONSEQUENCE LOSING THREE QUARTERS OF VOLUME

	Present £	Prices Doubled £
Sales	100	200
75% Lost	—	(150)
Net Sales	100	50
Cost of Sales	75	19 (¼ of 75)
Gross Margin	25	31

Assuming that labour costs as well as material costs can be scaled back *pro rata*, which ought to be possible given sufficient advanced notice, the company is in fact 24% better off in terms of real gross margin, real income, than before! This happens at only one-quarter of the volume. Working capital requirement has been more than halved; and there is scope to cut overheads as well for a business that is now only one quarter its original size.

Price Capacity

No-one was actually suggesting that the company *should* go so far as to actually double its prices. It merely illustrated the enormous unsuspected room for manoeuvre there was in taking a tougher line on prices.

So we then got down to looking at the individual contracts that made up the most recent month's sales (January) to see what scope there was for putting up prices, even if it meant losing contracts.

Analysing the Solution

The MD could broadly estimate material costs and labour hours in each of the jobs that went into sales for a typical month, which he was therefore asked to do. (The reason for using *hours* rather than labour *costs* will emerge shortly.) By summing total material used and total hours worked, comparison could be made with the overall figures per the monthly accounts, using the following layout:

Figure 38

XYZ LIMITED. ANALYSIS OF SALES FOR MONTH OF JANUARY, 1982

Contract	Sales	Materials	Labour Hours	Labour £	Cost of Sales	Gross Margin £	Gross Margin %
	£	£		£	£	£	%
A	3,000	1,500	400	1,000	2,500	500	16.7
B	500	100	40	100	200	300	60.0
C	1,400	400	120	300	700	700	50.0
D	5,000	1,800	400	1,000	2,800	2,200	44.0
E	500	200	40	100	300	200	40.0
TOTAL	10,400	4,000	1,000	2,500	6,500	3,900	37.5 Av.
Slippage	—	250	400	1,000	1,250	(1,250)	(12.1)Av.
Per Accounts	10,400	4,250	1,400	3,500	7,750	2,650	25.4 Av.

The layout is a more detailed restatement of the first part of the standard Profit and Loss Account viz:

Figure 39

XYZ LIMITED. OVERALL GROSS PROFIT FOR MONTH OF JANUARY, 1982

	£
Sales	10,400
Cost of Sales	
Materials	4,250
Labour	3,500 (1400 hrs @ £2.50 per hour)
	7,750
Gross Margin	2,650
GM%	25.4

The material side tied up well, as would be expected, with only £250 of raw material unaccounted for, showing that that aspect of the pricing was reasonably accurate.

As will be seen, the hours side, however, showed a large disparity: 1,000 "productive" hours in sales compared with 1,400 hours paid for. Subsequent investigation tracked down the problem to production that had not previously been identified, to some extent to do with the design of the product itself.

Note the concentration on labour hours, not cost. Hours is a much more straight-forward concept and leads directly on to a number of other useful exercises, from production planning on one hand to sales pricing on the other, as will be explained.

Gross Margin Target

It will be noticed from Figure 38 that gross margin totalled £2,650 on sales of £10,400. The overheads of the particular business in question were £5,500 so gross margin had *somehow* to be doubled. But remember this can be done just as well by losing some of even the existing level of business, however modest, as by trying to build up more volume.

Room for Manoeuvre on Sales Pricing

Because of this, the room for manoeuvre is, as we have seen already, substantially greater than first appearances suggest.

Examining Individual "Jobs"

The first thing to notice is that Contract D was providing nearly 60% of the total gross margin, gross margin being what really matters, so obviously great care is needed in making *any* price moves, for if that contract were lost it would be very serious.

More normally a large contract like this would be earning, say, £1,000 (20%) to £1,250 (25%) gross margin, a useful contributor to profit, a real set back if lost. Conversely because it involves a relatively high level of sales turnover even a small percentage price rise would have quite a big effect on total gross margin. So *some* very careful attempts could, indeed should, be made to ease up the price, perhaps in small frequent amounts progressively over a period of months.

Suppose this resulted in another 4% or £200 successfully being added to the price. This of course goes straight through into gross margin:

Figure 40a

CONTRACT D

	Sales	Mats.	Labour		Cost of Sales	Gross Margin	
	£	£	Hours	£	£	£	%
Before	5,000	1,800	400	1,000	2,800	2,200	44.0
After	5,200	1,800	400	1,000	2,800	2,400	46.1

Conversely, look at the two apparently minute contracts in sales terms, B and E. They are contributing usefully to profits, but what would happen if *their* prices were doubled? They are probably one-off, trial jobs anyway where price is of little consideration. Additionally the company may have incurred considerable overheads in terms of design, etc. costs, that the customer would expect, indeed be happy, to pay for. So you probably could add another few hundred pounds to the price of both B and E and get away with it, all of which, of course, again goes straight through into gross margin.

Figure 40b

CONTRACT B

	Sales	Mats.	Labour		Cost of Sales	Gross Margin	
	£	£	Hours	£	£	£	%
Before	500	100	40	100	200	300	60.0
After	700	100	40	100	200	500	71.4

Figure 40c

CONTRACT E

	Sales	Mats.	Labour		Cost of Sales	Gross Margin	
	£	£	Hours	£	£	£	%
Before	500	200	40	100	300	200	40.0
After	1,000	200	40	100	300	700	70.0

Contract C is probably a smallish order of regular product to a new customer unconnected with your main market. You can therefore experiment and gamble to see just how "price-hard" your product is in general, going on putting up the price to such customers until they start genuinely crying-off on grounds of cost. You will often surprise yourself how far you can go with this experiment before cut-off happens, particularly if the product is well designed and styled and provides your customer with quality, value for money, reliability and service.

Figure 40d

CONTRACT C

	Sales	Mats.	Labour		Cost of Sales	Gross Margin	
	£	£	Hours	£	£	£	%
Before	1,400	400	120	300	700	700	50.0
After	1,800	400	120	300	700	1,100	61.1

Finally what about contract A? Because of the high turnover it is cluttering up your works and appreciably raising your working capital requirements (which it will be remembered are related to turnover e.g. over three months' sales) for very little real reward. A 20% price rise would more than double gross margin, 30% would produce nearly three times more. So it is worth being "hard". If you lose the contract at those low margins you are better off without it and you can then release resources, for it takes up 40% of the productive payroll, forcing you to concentrate on something else. Similarly, if you are short of cash you might be able to save the £1,500 material cost and spend it more productively elsewhere. Business after all is about CASH.

Figure 40e

CONTRACT A

	Sales	Mats.	Labour (Hours)	Labour (£)	Cost of Sales	Gross Margin (£)	Gross Margin (%)
	£	£		£	£	£	%
Before	3,000	1,500	400	1,000	2,500	500	16.7
After	—	—	—	—	—	—	—

New Products

Finally what of the products not on the list? Can you develop a new product that would generate, say, £1,000 of gross margin more effectively than some of your existing range? If so quickly make the attempt. If these issues can be seen and appreciated well enough in advance, you *will* have the time, and you *will* have the resources, for remember a drop in turnover releases cash (from stocks and debtors) that can immediately be turned to other uses.

Figure 40f

CONTRACT F

	Sales	Mats.	Labour (Hours)	Labour (£)	Cost of Sales	Gross Margin (£)	Gross Margin (%)
	£	£		£	£	£	%
Before	—	—	—	—	—	—	—
After	2,000	500	200	500	1,000	1,000	50.0

Figure 41 shows, conceptually, what the Company was therefore setting out to try and do:

Figure 41

MARGIN UPLIFT

Contract		(1) Sales £	(2) Mats. £	(3) *Value Added £	(4) Labour Hrs	(5) Labour £	(6) *VA £/Hr	(7) GM £	(8) GM %
A		—	—	—	—	—	—	—	—
B	+	200	—	200	—	—	5.0	200	
	Old	500	100	400	40	100	10.0	300	71.4
C	+	400	—	400	—	—	3.3	400	
	Old	1,400	400	1,000	120	300	8.3	700	61.1
D	+	200	—	200	—	—	0.5	200	
	Old	5,000	1,800	3,200	400	1,000	8.0	2,200	46.1
E	+	500	—	500	—	—	12.5	500	
	Old	500	200	300	40	100	7.5	200	70.0
F	+	2,000	500	500	200	500	7.5	1,000	
	Old	—	—	—	—	—	—	—	50.0
TOTAL	+	3,300	500	2,800	200	500		2,300	
	Old	7,400	2,500	4,900	600	1,500		3,400	
		10,700	3,000	7,700	800	2,000	9.6	5,700	53.2 Av.

*Dealt with later in Chapter XII

Comparing Figure 41 with Figure 38 it will be seen loss of Contract A reduced total gross margin from £3,900 to £3,400 but £2,300 extra gross margin has been won, £1,300 from existing products, £1,000 from new. Total raw material costs are down from £4,000 to £3,000 and there are still 200 hours of labour capacity to play with (800 hours against 1,000 previously).

The Outcome

So what did happen to the company in question? Did it survive? Here is the October result compared with January:

Figure 42

XYZ LIMITED. EFFECT OF MARGIN IMPROVEMENT OVER A NINE MONTH PERIOD

	Jan. '82 £'000	Oct. '82 £'000	Improvements £'000	
Sales	10.4	15.0	3.0 *1.6	27.9% up by value
Cost of Sales	7.7	8.9	1.2 0.4	15.6% up by volume
Gross Margin	2.7	6.1	3.0	126.0% up
Overheads	5.5	6.0	0.5	by value
Profit/(Loss)	(2.8)	0.1	2.9	
Gross Margin %	26.0%	40.7%		
Breakeven	21.1	14.7		

*Of the £4,600 improvement in sales value, £3,000 resulted from improved pricing, 27.9% up; £1,600 from improved volume 15.6% up.

Stop Press

Five months later the Company was comfortably into profit:

Figure 43

XYZ LIMITED. IMPROVEMENT OVER A 14 MONTH PERIOD

	Jan. '82 £'000	Oct. '82 £'000	Mar. '83 £'000
Sales	10.4	15.0	27.9
Costs of Sales	7.7	8.9	15.4
Gross Margin	2.7	6.1	12.5
Overheads	5.5	6.0	6.3
Profit/(Loss)	(2.8)	0.1	6.2
Gross Margin %	26.0%	40.7%	44.8%
Breakeven	21.1	14.7	14.1

As turnover edged up past breakeven point healthy profits began to emerge and the management were particularly skillful in ensuring that further improvements in margin occurred to cover the further modest increases in overhead associated with increasing turnover.

Given the state of the Company in January, 1982, profits of £2,000 per month seemed beyond the dreams of reason, even survival itself. Yet 14 months later *three times* that figure were beginning to be achieved with the promise of better to come.

An analysis of selected jobs in the sales mix for March, compared to Figures 38 and 41 is illustrative:

Figure 44

ANALYSIS OF SELECTED SALES CONTRACTS

	Sales	Mats.	V/A	Labour Hrs	£	VA/Hr	Gross Margin £	%
Contract B								
Before	500	100	400	40	100	10.0	300	60.0
After	1,000	200	800	50	125	16.0	675	67.5
Contract C								
Before	1,400	400	1,000	120	300	8.3	700	50.0
After	1,700	300	1,400	100	250	14.0	1,150	67.6
Contract E								
Before	500	200	300	40	100	7.5	200	40.0
After	900	200	700	40	100	17.5	600	66.7
Contract F								
Before	—	—	—	—	—	—	—	—
After	2,700	1,400	1,300	80	200	16.3	1,100	40.7

etc.

Here we have the beneficial effects not just of more resolute pricing but, as discussed in Chapters XIII to XV, improved production and product design, which can result in lower labour and material costs, as in Contract C. Alternatively, where say quality has been improved, although resulting in *higher* labour and material costs, it can provide greatly enhanced opportunities to raise prices, as in Contract B.

"Prices" *v* "Volume" Sensitivity in Market

A 27.9% average price rise was achieved (figure 42), which, far from resulting in a *drop* in volume, was associated with a 15.6% actual *increase* in volume, partly explained by bringing in new products and partly by the generally tougher way in which the business was now being run, which seems to have favourably influenced customers' confidence.

Sensitivity of Sales *v* Gross Profit

Note that the combination of 27.9% higher prices and 15.6 % more volume produced no less than 126% increase in gross margin. So real income increased by this spectacular amount.

Closing the Breakeven Gap

Note also how the breakeven gap had been closed. It looked an impossible task at sales of £10,400 to drive turnover up to £21,200 in a depressed market. But it was not necessary. By improving the *quality* of earnings, breakeven point by October had been pulled down from £21,100 to £14,700. So sales did not have to rise so far, from £10,400 to only £15,000. The problem looked much more containable on that basis.

"Weak" *v* "Strong" Gross Margins

Note how weak the company was when operating at 26% margin and how much it has strengthened in getting to over 40%. It meant, too, that as sales edged up past £20,000 a profit of over £2,000 per month was beginning to be generated. Not a fortune, but a rate of £24,000 per year, more in fact, than the whole overdraft in this particular case.

"Survival"

This was achieved for a Company where as recently as January, management were about to close it down. The market was scarcely better, most of the 15% rise was probably no more than inflation anyway, and the market was still very much "bumping along the bottom".

"Success"

Already by October, a new and vigorous Company was emerging despite all the difficulties, which was scaled back, tailored, and well able to live within the reduced market conditions it faced. It was just as well. Reduced market conditions can be permanent; or at least a management team would be most unwise to act on any other assumption.

The MD was in his 50s and had been in business all his life. It could so easily have ended in disaster. He would have been left with nothing. As it was he emerged with his self-respect intact, his self-esteem intact, indeed much enhanced, and with a real feeling of achievement. He admitted "to having had a good many more sleepless nights" as the regular monthly figures came through, but that very process of knowledge enabled him to start winning, and winning against all the odds. For the first time, perhaps, he had a full "gut-feel" for business issues.

The Learning Process

But he needed to be shown the way. How many other companies like this are there in the British economy? Or sadly, are no longer, just because they did not have that "feel" or did not have it in time?

Chapter XII

VALUE ADDED

The last Chapter leads onto another valuable concept, Value Added and Value Added per Hour.

Treatment of Labour Costs

Labour can now, for full accuracy, be treated separately as neither a fixed cost nor a variable cost. It is then possible to increase or decrease production in direct sympathy with the ebbs and flows, set-backs and opportunities of the business, just indeed as has been done for sales. This is no more than what must happen anyway if the business is to be kept accurately dovetailed to the opportunities and set-backs of the market place itself.

Definition of Value Added

Value Added is sales price less all direct sales costs (freight, duty, sales discounts and commissions, etc.) and material costs. It is the "contribution" not, as before, just to overheads and profit, but to overheads, profit and labour costs.

Definition of Value Added per Hour

If value added on one hand and labour plus overhead costs on the other are divided by productive hours (i.e. something less than total hours paid for, to allow for idle time, holidays, sickness, etc.) then *income per productive hour* on one hand can be compared with *costs per productive hour* on the other. The comparison is often revealing.

Let's insert the income value added in the sales analysis given in Figure 38 to produce Figure 45.

Tracking Down Labour and Materials Slippage

The first point to note is that only 1,000 hours out of 1,400 are "Productive", namely 71%. It ought to be possible, by analysing more precisely where the hours are going, through a job card and time-sheet system dealing only in HOURS, to improve this to at least 80%. Another 112 productive hours worked on jobs producing an added value of, say, £10 per hour, would bring in an extra £1,120. Incidentally a "productive" hour (as distinguishable for instance from an overhead salary) is any hour that can be identified to a particular job, including any hour that physically helps move work one step nearer despatch, including testing, inspection and quality control.

Figure 45

XYZ LIMITED. ANALYSIS OF SALES FOR THE MONTH OF JANUARY, 1982

Contract	[1] Sales	[2] *Mats.	[3] Value Added	[4] Labour	[5] Labour	[6] VA/Prod. Hour	[7] Gross Margin	[8] Gross Margin
	£	£	£	H's	£	£/Hr	£	%
A	3,000	1,500	1,500	400	1,000	3.75	500	16.7
B	500	100	400	40	100	10.00	300	60.0
C	1,400	400	1,000	120	300	8.33	700	50.0
D	5,000	1,800	3,200	400	1,000	8.00	2,200	44.0
E	500	200	300	40	100	7.50	200	40.0
TOTAL	10,400	4,000	6,400	1,000	2,500	6.40	3,900	37.5
Slippage	—	250	(250)	[400]	1,000	0.25	(1,250)	(12.1)
Per Accounts	10,400	4,250	6,150	[1,400]	3,500	6.15	2,650	25.4

*Directly variable sales costs (freight, commissions, duty, etc.) are here included with material costs for brevity of illustration as they were e.g. in Figure 38. Normally they would form a separate column.

And the cost side:

Figure 46a

XYZ LIMITED. ANALYSIS OF COSTS FOR THE MONTH OF JANUARY, 1982
(From Figures 42 and 45)

	[9] £	[10] Productive Hours	[11] £/Hour
Productive labour	2,500	1,000	[(2.50)]
Unproductive labour	1,000	[400]	[(2.50)]
Materials "waste"	250		
Overheads	5,500		
TOTAL	9,250	1,000	9.25 Av.

Income per Hour *v* Costs per Hour

Secondly, costs per hour at £9.25 are clearly out of line with Income per hour, ranging from £3.75 to £10.00, an average of only £6.40. Only *one* job Contract B is producing more than £9.25 per hour. All the rest are producing less and in the case of contract A abysmally so.

Need to Close Gap

Unless the company can achieve a sales value added per hour better than its cost rate per hour, it is clearly not going to make a profit. There are only two ways of doing so:

(1) By bringing down cost per hour, column [11];
(2) By pushing up value added per hour [6].

How to Close Gap

There are two ways of achieving (1):

(3) Cut overhead costs, reduce material and labour "wastage", reduce rates of pay per hour (i.e. cut overtime, reduce bonuses and commission, etc.) [9];
(4) Increase number of hours worked [4] [10].

On (4), suppose 4 extra employees were taken on, producing another 700 hours gross, 500 hours net (productive) per month. The cost side would then look as shown in Figure 46b.

It is clearly no good doing this unless the necessary contracts are available. But if sales are very price-sensitive it might be easier to win, say, 1,500 hours of business at £9.00 per hour than, say, 1,000 hours at £11.00 per hour (allowing for profit).

Figure 46b

	COSTS £	Hrs	£/Hr
Productive labour:			
Old	2,500	1,000	[2.50]
New	1,250	500	[2.50]
Un-Productive labour:			
Old	1,000	[400]	[2.50]
New	500	[200]	[2.50]
Materials waste (say)	250		
Overheads (say)	6,000		
TOTAL	11,500	1,500	7.67 Av.

resulting in a valuable cost reduction from £9.25/hr to £7.67/hr.

Improving Income/Hour

Turning now to the income side, again there are two ways of improving value added per hour:

(5) Increase value added in money terms [3];

(6) Reduce hourly content of a job, the hours taken to produce a job [4].

Value Added can obviously be increased by:

(7) Raising sales prices [1];

(8) Reducing material content in a job [2];

(9) Reducing directly variable sales costs (delivery etc.) in a job [2].

There are three aspects to (8):

(10) Organise and run the production side more efficiently, or even completely redesign production, to reduce material and labour use and waste;

(11) Harder-nosed buying to reduce raw material prices;

(12) Redesign product to lower material content or substitute cheaper materials for more expensive.

Reducing Sales Costs

On (9), unpleasant surprises sometimes emerge when the figures are grouped in the way envisaged. For instance at the moment you may be showing *trade discounts* to customers, say 25% reduction in price for bulk deliveries above a certain level, under overheads. Include them instead under direct costs and the 40% gross margin you thought you were getting comes down to 15%.

Similarly, the sales force may have a *bonus incentive scheme* based on turnover. If given at all, incentives should be related to gross margin (or value added or value added above a certain level, above say breakeven point), not to turnover, to avoid the very pitfalls mentioned here. Every 10% thus given away reduces the gross margin by a similar amount i.e. brings a 40% margin down to 30%.

A *cash discount* for prompt payment (again a cost related to turnover) reduces gross margin. Unusually *expensive delivery costs* may not fully be taken into account in arriving at gross margin (including duty, etc.). Watch for any cost that you would not have incurred had you not handled the product, *giveaway sales literature*, *special packaging* (ordinary packing should be included under materials), *explanatory brochures*, *additional costs of winning the contract*, *free display material*, *stands*, etc.

Strictly you should also include items like the cost of all *design work* done for the client, additional *inspection procedures*, additional *testing procedures* and so on.

A Typical Blunder

By failing to link cost and reward properly, the most bizarre mistakes can sometimes be made.

One film distribution company were jubilant when they obtained exclusive rights, after some very hard bargaining, for a particularly successful film. It was in such popular demand they found they could sell it to the cinemas for around 20% of takings, compared to the normal 10%. It went like a bomb, outlet after outlet taking it up.

Normally a distributor would only be able to hire out a film for, say, 12% of takings. With a standard 8% of takings being payable to the producer, normal margin would be 4%. But with the normal margin having been trebled from 4% to 12% they were in for a bonanza. Or so they thought.

Only later was it discovered that someone had contracted to pay the producer 25% of takings, instead of the normal 8%, in order to obtain the rights in the face of fierce competition. Try as they would they could not stop the film's run-away success . . . It went on for years. Hitting all-time records. So did the loss-making.

Don't fall into the same trap

Ensure that in fixing prices you bring into account *all* turnover-related payments (such as bonus schemes, discounts for prompt payment or cash, discounts for quantity, special give-aways to attract business, design-work, etc.).

That does not mean you cannot take on a trial contract at perhaps a deliberate loss to open up a new area of business. "Loss-leading", as it is termed, correctly used, is a most valuable part of the business scene. But you must calculate well in advance the precise extent of the loss and all the additional costs it is going to burden the business with.

Even if it is a question of "we have no other choice", as happened to Rolls Royce with the RB211, you *must* know the precise extent of the commitment, however unpalatable. Somehow it has got to be financed (if it isn't, you go bust). The attempt to raise sufficient finance, whether or not successful, cannot even be made until you know the size of the problem. Only then can minds begin to be focussed, too, on whether there might be other ways of achieving the same ends, but in a less dangerous fashion.

Future Commitments need Watching too

Finally, watch very carefully for *future* commitments associated with a contract, such as guarantees or sale-or-return obligations, penalties for late delivery or maintenance contracts. They, too, have to come off the margin to the extent that they are not reimbursed out of future income from that same job.

Quantify, Quantify, Quantify

Murphy's law being what it is "if anything can go wrong it will and even if it can't it might", *nothing* should be left to chance. It is no good turning a blind eye, hoping it won't happen, being afraid to calculate the full extent of commitment for fear of what it might show you (or your colleagues). You must know precisely, however daunting the knowledge. Knowledge is certainty in business. Forewarned is forearmed. Given the facts, however unpalatable, there is usually a way . . .

But until the facts *are* available, right and fully assembled, the process cannot even start. Even worse is the case where you have only half the facts thinking you have them all; you then go forward on the wrong assumptions and therefore make the wrong decisions. Knowledge must be complete, which is not the same, of course, as being fully accurate. Quick, broadbrush knowledge and therefore understanding is altogether more preferable to the precise picture being available 6 months later. In business, as in politics, even a week is a long time.

Danger of Large Contracts

Significantly, it is often the large contract going wrong that is likely to overwhelm a business more than a number of small contracts faltering or indeed absence of work altogether. This is because the "momentum" of a large contract carries all before it. You cannot stop it if things go wrong, only attempt to cóntrol its general direction. So you must identify well in advance all the parameters that attach to it and keep a very close watch over each, from day one. This particularly applies to any cost that is turnover related. Commissions, penalties for late delivery, etc. are all, by definition, largest for the largest contract.

Don't become Overdependent on One Contract, One Product, One Customer

For this reason, try and avoid having more than, say, 30% of your business with any one customer or in any one product line, however enticing the prospect of still larger orders.

We may seem to have strayed some way from the discussion on value added, but in fact we have not. If you relate all the factors just mentioned back to value added and gross margin, and keep on monitoring changes for example as a large contract progresses, it will give you a mind's eye view of the significance of those changes, enabling you to rank them in order of importance and to control them accordingly.

Raw Material Savings—(Item (8) on Page 114)

Again the arithmetic can be strange and needs following through. Returning for a moment to the techniques for saving raw material in production, in the plastics company given as a case history in Chapter IV, radio-active scanning equipment costing £100,000 per line was available to scan the sheet emerging from the extruders to control its thickness to a more uniform degree. The sheet overall could then be made fractionally thinner without the danger of "thin" spots.

Calculation showed that on average it would save 4% of material cost and therefore improve gross margins by 4%, which clearly was not worth doing.

Or was it? 4% improvement on the margins of the time (15%+) was enormous. Secondly, output per thermoforming line was around £4m p.a. of which material cost, pre the restructuring, was around half. 4% of £2m is £80,000. The equipment, even at a capital cost of £100,000 per unit, thus paid for itself within 15 months. After that, each line, of which there were four, contributed £80,000 to profit, the benefit increasing annually with increasing raw material prices, which were oil-based.

Remember we are looking at gross margin, value added (all the techniques mentioned in this chapter apply equally to both, incidentally) not looking at sales turnover. A small percentage change in the latter can be equivalent to a big percentage change in the two former, where the *real* income of the business lies.

Value Added per Productive Hour

Finally, and most important of all, once all possibilities for improving value added have been fully utilised (and you will see there are many) the possibilities on the income side are still not exhausted, for what matters is value added *per productive hour*.

In Figure 45 only one job at £10/hr is producing enough to cover costs of £9.25. Even then it is only *just* doing so. All the others are producing less.

Improving Value Added per Hour

But supposing by:

(1) Redesigning the product to make it quicker to assemble;

(2) Re-organising and redesigning the production process itself;

a way could be found of making product A, with a present value added £3.75/hr (barely above *direct* labour cost) in only 100 hours instead of 400. Value added in money terms would be unchanged [3] but value added per hour [6] would leap fourfold to £15 and become the best job in the sales mix. Ugly Duckling into Swan as it were.

This would then also release 300 hours of productive time for something else. If there were little other work available, at least two people could be laid off until further work did come in, saving up to £1,000 per month in costs. But hopefully some quick other work *could* be found. With costs already covered prices could be slashed to get the business. The full value added would come through as profit.

The Nation's Resources
Technical ingenuity is one of our nation's great resources. In the production of ideas Britain arguably leads the world. If the same skill and ingenuity could come to be harnessed to value engineering as well, like our foreign competitors, we could be world beaters in this area too. A significantly larger number of really strong companies would emerge, capable of taking on all-comers, a subject that is enlarged on in Chapter XV.

Racal
Racal, for instance, sells tape recorders to the Japanese which are used in their airports. Racal's success lies partly in some very fine technical ideas, but mainly in the business-engineering that goes into arriving at the design of the finished product, and identifying and linking what the market wants with a product designed to meet market need and produce high value added, high gross margin (60% to 80% one suspects) and high value added per hour.

A Case History
Returning to the theme of value added, the author recently introduced a very able engineer, running his own business, with a large order book but problems in getting work out of the door, to the value added per hour concept.

The overall cost of running the company was, typically, £10/hr. It had some very good contracts with value addeds ranging up to £40/hr. But the bulk of the work was in long-running, bread-and-butter lines at around £5/hr to £7/hr (often longer-running than was intended!). Something had to be done fairly fast.

There seemed little that could be done about the £5/hr work. It would just have to be worked off. With the order book standing at £0.75m and output stubbornly refusing to rise above £50,000 a month, this meant a timescale of at least 15 months.

There was just one small problem. Cash was likely to run out in the next 6 weeks. Additionally, in order to meet customers' delivery deadlines the work *had* to be completed within not more than 5 months, serious delays were occuring and customers were becoming restive.

The Managing Director, when confronted with the problem, suddenly said:

"I can do something about the £5/hr work."

"You *can?*" "What?" "Surely you can't put up sales prices for orders already in-house?"

"No. That would do quite unacceptable damage to our established customers. In any case, we are up at the top end of the range already."

"Then what?"

"I could redesign the circuit layout to take 40 minutes to put together instead of 1½ hours."

"Yes."

"That would not affect value added of course, but it *would* double value added per *hour*, wouldn't it?"

"Yes."

"It should be possible, given the effort."

"If you can reduce the time taken to make the product from 1½ hours to 40 minutes why in the * * * * didn't you do so in the first place?"

"I never perceived the need. The product sells for £20, has a £13 material content and £4 labour, which seems little enough compared with the overall price. There seemed no obvious reason to devote valuable time and effort towards improving it still more. Indeed the reverse. It could become a question of rapidly diminishing returns. It's a fairly major task, not quite as bad as designing the product itself in the first place, but of the same order. It doesn't really seem worth while for such small gains even now; although I accept the value added per hour is doubled."

"Small gains?"

"£2. The labour cost saved."

"And?"

"Well, what else?"

"What are you going to do with the 40 minutes saved?"

"Run more product. . . . Oh, bloody hell, I could run *twice* as much couldn't I?"

"Yes."

"Through the same cost base?"

"Yes."

"In the same time as it takes to run one unit now."

"Yes."

"I would gain the full value added of £7 on the second unit for no extra labour or overhead cost?"

"Yes."

"Which would come straight through into cash flow and profits?"

"Yes."

"I can *double* the productive capacity of the factory for no extra cost?"

"Yes."

"Particularly if I could also redesign the production process itself to further speed things up."

"Yes."

"And it would be worth spending quite a lot of time, effort and money on doing so."

"Yes."

"I've never quite looked at things this way before. One thing we will do immediately is amalgamate the R & D, Production and Design teams into one unit, with each member capable of covering all aspects."

"Good thinking."

"All sorts of possibilities open up."

Indeed they did. Within three months:

Output had jumped from £50,000 to £140,000 per month.

Monthly losses of £15,000 had transformed into monthly profits of £10,000.

Delivery promises to customers started to be honoured.

Customers breathed a huge sigh of relief, for *their* production lines were tied into the Company's delivery schedules. They started to re-order, if anything at enhanced levels. Up to £250,000 per month.

UK Sourcing

A feature here was that one of the customers, a major multi-national in the electronics industry, was presently sourcing supplies from three countries, the US, Germany and the UK. It wanted to place more business in the UK but with UK firms all 3 to 4 months late on deliveries, which seemed a general feature of the scene, they dared not. As soon as this particular company speeded up and showed it could begin to meet on-line requirements, the multi-national were only too pleased to source more work with them in the UK, to bring the UK closer to quota.

"We can't afford it"

The workforce increased from 38 to 54 and, a sub-contractor's from 19 to 30. No longer was there the argument "we can't afford it".

It was realised the company could not not afford it, with prospective income of £10/hr to £40/hr in prospect (a reflection of the spread of work in the order book) against the extra cost of £2/hr.

Finding enough money for R & D had always been a problem. R & D had been running at around 7% of turnover. Now it could be increased to around 15%, the proper level for an electronics company. This enabled the company to accelerate considerably the production of new designs, the next generation of product, R & D, etc., keeping them to the forefront, indeed ahead of even the most intense Far Eastern competition.

All Hell let Loose

Next time we visited the company, all hell had been let loose. The MD had called for an exact comparison to be made of all hours paid for, per the clock cards, with productive hours for the past nine months.

There were 8,000 hours unaccounted for. The MD had mentally registered that each hour lost had cost the business, in lost cash flow and profits, £10 to £40 per hour. Say £160,000 in the nine months!

Tiny Slippages worth Chasing

He began to appreciate that *tiny* slippages had quite disproportionate effects and *were* worth spending a good deal of time and effort tracking down.

For instance it was discovered that sometimes those at the work-benches didn't have a complete kit of parts to start on. ¼hr or ½hr could be lost. Up to then this would have been "costed," if identified at all, at a mere £2/hr. Now it was being costed at at least £20!

Personal Considerations

At one time the MD was seriously thinking of moving aside and bringing in an experienced outside MD to run the business. One was in fact found. Naturally he wanted 30% of the company, which with great reluctance, was accepted. The Production Director, another very able engineer and also a founder shareholder like the MD, found himself and his job under threat too.

However, as the weeks went by and the MD began to acquire a full "feel" for the issues, including better control of debtors and other cash flow aspects, he was asked:

"Do you *really* want a professional MD to move in?"

"I am beginning to wonder. Four months ago I was an Engineer. Now I am a Businessman."

In the event, there was no need to invite the new MD in, much to the relief of all concerned (except of course the new MD himself, for it was an attractive company and he very much wanted to get his hands on it).

Happily the same was true of the Production Director. The Company achieved its record £140,000 output level just before Easter.

"How do you feel? Do you feel absolutely exhausted" (those were not quite the words) "or exhilarated?" It was an important test.

"Tired, but exhilarated. It has been one of the most stimulating four weeks of my life."

"Block" freed

There was no question from then on of either of them stepping down or moving aside. The "block" on progress had been freed, entirely by their own efforts. In the process they had "found" themselves as businessmen.

Sub-consciously all who dealt with the company, workforce, customers, suppliers, financial backers, sensed it and began to relax. A powerful company was emerging, driving forwards to success, quietly confident.

The Need

In the main what was needed was to get the perception across, the concept of being able to reduce a whole business to income value added per hour on one hand and cost per hour on the other and to introduce simplified methods of good financial and cash flow control. The rest the MD and Production Director did of their own accord, their own engineering brilliance playing a crucial and key role.

"Our job isn't making steel, it's making money." "The product is not important. Its price/cost/demand relationship is."

Chapter XIII

SALES PRICING

Method

Once the direct cost side has been reduced to just the three basic elements:

1) **Material Content**
2) **Direct Sales Costs**
3) **Productive Hours**

certain valuable exercises open up.

Order Value-Added per Hour

Firstly, you can rapidly calculate the value added per hour in your existing Order Book. Orders can be analysed in exactly the same way as sales were in the last chapter. Suppose you originally arrived at the sales price of contract A on the basis of the following material, direct labour cost and hour assumptions:

Figure 47

CONTRACT A—ESTIMATED OUT-TURN

	£
Sales Value	2,600
Less: Material and Direct Labour Costs	1,200
Value Added	1,400
Hours	200
Value Added/Hour	7.00

This is the *estimated* outcome of the Contract.

Checking the Accuracy of Estimates for Pricing Purposes

When a contract is "Completed" the two sets of figures can be compared side by side:

Figure 48

XYZ LIMITED. SALES FOR THE MONTH OF JANUARY 1982

	Estimate	Actual	Better (Worse)
	£	£	£
Sales Value	2,600	3,000	400
Materials, etc.	1,200	1,500	(300)
Value Added	1,400	1,500	100
Productive Hours	200	400	(200)
Value Added per Hour	£7.00	£3.75	(£3.25)

What went wrong? There are only two possibilities:
   (1) The assumptions used for pricing purposes were, by any standards, over-optimistic;
   (2) The assumptions were in fact rational, soundly-based and attainable, but failed to be achieved through poor management, inadequate production planning, poor supervision, failure to motivate the workforce properly and so on;

or a combination of both.

Tracking Down the Reason

It is clearly important to establish which reason is right. For instance it may be possible by introducing different work-practices, changed production sequences, bonus incentive schemes, etc., to get production hours down from 400 hours to, say, 300 hours. Future estimates for the same job would then be lifted from 200 hours to 300.

Events tend to change so rapidly in the typical company that **this comparison exercise needs to be done regularly as a matter of routine. The most convenient way is to analyse *all* sales monthly in the manner outlined.**

This provides you with constantly updated "feed-back", the yardstick you must have to establish fully what is happening on a day-to-day basis.

Job Hour Estimates will Initially be very Inaccurate

This process will particularly be necessary where, initially, the estimate of the number of hours likely to be taken for a job can only be a broad guess until experience has built up. In this context you may know of the 80%

curve discovered during aircraft manufacture in the last war. Every time output doubles, costs tend to reduce by 20% as experience builds up. So the number of hours taken in a job is not a fixed, permanent, feature. Initially, actual time taken will be well over estimate, gradually coming down to estimate and then eventually falling below it (depending on how well the estimate is pitched in the first place) and this is happening over all jobs.

Fixing Sales Prices

The converse of the methods just mentioned, of course, is that once you have established accurate "bench-marks" for job:

> Material costs
> Direct sales costs
> Productive hours

you can PRICE accurately.

"Accurately" means in two senses:

> being *certain* of the margin contained in the product and
>
> knowing how far you can go in darting in and out of the market place at selected prices to win this, that, or the other order.

The last aspect goes to the very heart of giving your company, whatever its size, the barrow-boy ability to "trade" in its market place more or less whatever the climate, good, bad or indifferent. This forms such a large subject, however, that its potential can only briefly be hinted at in a book of this nature.

Back-of-the-Envelope Pricing

Looking first at productive hours, once you have decided what value-added per hour to go for, pricing can be done on the back-of-an-envelope, on the spur of the moment if necessary. It enables you to react and take reliable decisions there and then as an enquiry comes in through the door or on the phone.

Suppose as your starting point you need to achieve a value added of at least £15/hr to "cover" costs of £9.25/hr (Figure 46a, Chapter XII) and leave room for profits and slippage.

Bench-Mark Pricing

This means Contract A in figure 45 would need to be priced at a bench-mark level of £6,000, found as follows:

Figure 49

BENCH-MARK SELLING PRICE

	£
Materials and Sales Costs	1,500
Labour 300 hours @ £15	4,500
Bench-Mark Selling Price	**6,000**

which assumes the contract *should* take 300 hours not 400.

Lower-Limit Pricing

If your pricing procedures can be made really accurate by introducing the measures outlined at the start of this chapter into the monthly accounts as a matter of routine, you can avoid the uncertainty and imprecision of allowing *anything* for slippage. You can then confidently price down to, say, £12/hr, giving a lower-limit price of £5,100:

Figure 50

LOWEST SELLING PRICE

	£
Materials, etc.	1,500
Labour 300 @ £12	3,600
Lowest Selling Price	**5,100**

Upper Limit Pricing

Alternatively, if a number of specialities have been built into the product which the customer really wants and is prepared to pay for, you might go up to £40/hr:

Figure 51

HIGHEST SELLING PRICE

	£
Materials, etc.	1,500
Labour 300 @ £40	12,000
Highest Selling Price	**13,500**

Flexibility

The flexibility, simplicity, understanding and speed this system provides is considerable, as may be appreciated

Barrow-Boy Trading

Now for the real barrow-boy "trading" side, where the volume aspect also influences price. By VOLUME of course is meant HOURS.

The more hours a company works in a month for a given overhead, the lower the cost per hour; the fewer it works, the higher the cost per hour. It was shown in the last chapter how by working an extra 500 productive hours average costs could be reduced from £9.25/hr to £7.67/hr (Figure 46b).

High Volume, Low Price

If it is easier to sell 1,500 hours at, say, £10/hr (allowing for profit) than 1,000 hours at, say, £12.50/hr, then clearly the former should be chosen.

Low Volume, High Price

But the reverse may be true. You may have such a good product that you can charge £30/hr for it, but there is only demand for 450 hours worth a month.

Figure 52

PROFIT (LOSS) AT £30/hr

	£
Income 450 × £30	13,500
Costs (Figure 46a)	*9,250
Profit	4,250

*deliberately avoiding lay-offs despite the reduced hours sold.

Cut-Off Point

Going for low volume and high price in this way would be very much worth doing. In fact the cut-off point in this case is any combination of value added and hours that produces a value added of say £11,000 (allowing for profit) viz:

Figure 53

ALTERNATIVE SELLING PRICES TO PRODUCE £11,000 VALUE ADDED

	Hrs	VA/Hr	VA£
Alternative 1	1,000	11.00	11,000
" 2	800	13.75	11,000
" 3	500	22.00	11,000
" 4	250	44.00	11,000

etc.

Production-Gap-Filling

Now the next scenario. Costs are £9,250 at 1,000 productive hours/month and you have already sold 500 hours at an average of £20/hr as follows:

Figure 54

PRODUCTION LOADING TO DATE

	Hrs	VA/Hr	VA£
Contract 1	150	20.0	3,000
" 2	100	40.0	4,000
" 3	250	12.0	3,000
Total to Date	500	20.0Av.	10,000

The costs of the remaining 500 hours are effectively "covered", so *any* selling price above £0.01/hr is all profit!

Loss-Leading

You might use this opportunity *for the particular production month in question* for a quick "loss-leading" foray into the market, at say £5/hr, to undercut the activities of a competitor and get a foot in the door with one of his, up-to-then, established customers. What Sales Director could resist such a veritable "licence to kill"? He must, however, get a sufficient base of high value work in place first. *That* is the incentive.

Hammering the Competition

It may indeed be "loss-leading" for your competitor if he has to follow you down to keep you out. If he succeeds in holding onto the business, you will at least have weakened his operation by forcing him to compete with you on your timing rather than his. Or if you do win the business, far from making a loss, you will make a very acceptable £2,500 profit out of it (500 hours at £5/hr).

Getting the Production Slots Right

But you have to get the production periods scrupulously right into which such activities slot, otherwise they may stray over into another period where for instance, the first 500 hours is earning only £10/hr. The total 1,000 hours then only earn £7,500 against costs of £9,250 and you are clearly in trouble, just the scenario you hope you have forced onto your competitor, if he succeeds in holding onto the business! Getting these production "slots" right forms the subject of the next chapter.

Selling "Extra" Hours

A different example. Total costs of £9,250 have been covered by selling 1,000 hours at £11/hr with no spare hours available. But an opportunity suddenly occurs in the market place to sell another 400 hours at £7/hr. Should you take it?

You can perhaps get your existing work-force to work overtime at, say, overtime rates of £4/hr against the £7/hr you are going to earn, producing a useful extra £1,200 profit.

Alternatively you can recruit temporary staff at say £2/hr like "outworkers" (housewives wanting to work only part-time, possibly even in their own homes) or put the work out to sub-contract, all of which will produce a useful extra profit.

Getting Production to "Support" Sales

Suppose a competitor is quoting £20,000 for a job with £9,000 material content and 1,300 hrs labour content. You would have to quote £23,300 to maintain, say, £11/hr.

With a little ingenuity, could material content be reduced to, say, £8,000 and hours to, say, 1,000 by reorganising production sequences, putting your best operators onto the job, special supervision, offering a £500 incentive bonus, etc., etc?

If so, you could quote £19,500, get the job *and* maintain £11/hr.

Simplicity and Accuracy

These pricing methods work because of their comparative simplicity, accuracy and speed. Everyone can quickly come to understand them and therefore respond to them. Properly used, they can be a powerful tool in heading a company in the right direction and on to success, in even the quite difficult markets.

Bread-and-Butter Lines

Yet another scenario. You run a business making specialist products for which you get very good prices, £30/hr or more, but the work tends to be lumpy, too much one month, not enough another. You want to man-up to handle the peaks in order to obtain maximum benefit and it is essential to do so anyway if you are to get the customer to trust you as a dependable supplier for the size of contract he wants.

Peaks and Troughs

But if you do so man-up, people may be standing around idle during the troughs on a scale of loss-making you simply cannot afford, but to lay people off would be most damaging in terms of forfeited staff loyalty, morale and continuity of the business. You want to keep the team together, the team who to date have so successfully got you down the 80% curve to give you that vital cost advantage over your competitors, but whose support would evaporate like mist in the morning sun if you laid them off.

The answer, if you can, is to forage round the market place for standard, "shelf", bread and butter lines. Here you have to price keenly to get the work, say down to £5/hr, but you may be able to obtain an extra 1,500 to 2,000 hours a month at these prices, offering the prospect of maintaining production month in and month out.

Bedrock Income

This will give you a "bedrock" income of, in this example, £7,500 to £10,000 per month, against related labour costs of £3,000 to £5,000. Net, this earns 40% to 45% of your target value added of £11,000 per month, leaving 55% to 60% to be picked-up from "specials" with another 500 to 1,000 hours.

Such a business will have a more stable "feel" to it, will be less prone to market adversity, more able to benefit from market opportunity, more able to make the quick in-and-out "killing".

Classic Mistake

Now we come to a classic mistake many companies seem to fall into at one time or another, which can wipe out the more "unfortunate" ones more or less overnight. [Incidentally there is no such thing as "bad luck" in business, only bad management. Conversely, the well-run company seems always to be so "lucky". Not luck, just sound organisation and farsightedness. The definition of bad-luck by the way is being marooned on an ice floe . . . and seeing the Titanic approaching.]

You need to generate say £9,250 of value added per month to cover all costs. You have a big contract, big enough perhaps to span several months. It is delivered. The customer rejects the work and under the terms of your contract you have to rectify it until specification is met, which may mean rebuilding major sections (the dangers of large contracts!).

Because you need the cash desperately, you put your entire workforce onto the remedial work. Within a short time you are indeed bust.

Spot the fatal flaw? You need to generate £9,250 per month, say 1,000 hours at £10/hr, to cover all costs, regardless. *Remedial work generates zero value added per hour.*

You must maintain 1,000 hours of production, at your usual margins, on other work, however great your commitments to your past customer (who will be a good deal "past" by now).

For such work you cannot afford to use hours costing effectively £10/hr. These very expensive hours *must* first be devoted to earning £10/hr or more, until all costs are covered. You *must* keep regular orders flowing in, you *must* keep regular product flowing out, regardless of all other preoccupations.

Having then at least ensured that the cash position is securely under-pinned by "covering" all regular costs, the remedial work can be done "on-the-margin" at overtime rates of, say, £5/hr or better still by increasing the workforce at, say, £3/hr.

Misconception about avoiding Cost Increases

Companies often don't do this because of the following entirely common-sense argument:

> "We are in desperate trouble already."

> "The last thing we can afford is to increase costs by taking on more people."

> "Let's get the remedial work done as fast as possible", usually incurring overtime in addition to normal rates, "so we can get paid for the contract".

> "Meanwhile the rest of the business will have to wait. No point in going out for more orders. We won't be able to deliver the work we have as it is because the staff are so fully committed on the remedial contract."

Avoiding such Mistakes

An all-too-understandable mistake, which hopefully introduction of the value added/hour concept will help you avoid. **You are dealing in relatives not absolutes. It is cost-in-relation-to-what? that matters, not cost by itself.**

You are far better off spending an extra £3/hr (on the remedial work) to earn £15/hr (on regular work) than by incurring no extra cost to earn £0/hr (on remedial work).

Chapter XIV

PRODUCTION

Concept of Hours

The concept of Hours is a useful, rapid, rule-of-thumb method for pricing and costing purposes and therefore for "trading" purposes, enabling you to compete effectively in the market-place, however strong the opposition, given a little ingenuity.

Measure of Volume and Timescale

But it has also, as already hinted, another useful characteristic. It is a measure of VOLUME, volume of production, volume of sales. It therefore enables you to plan production itself with speed, flexibility and accuracy.

Planning Production

To plan production each job in the Order Book can be planned forward into the weeks in which the work is to be done as follows:

Figure 55

PLANNING PRODUCTION FROM ORDERS—HOURS

Order	Total	Wk.1	Wk.2	Wk.3	Wk.4	Wk.5
A	400	—	50	150	200	—
B	40	—	—	—	40	—
C	120	120	—	—	—	—
D	400	200	200	—	—	—
E	40	—	40	—	—	—
F	400	—	—	200	100	100
G	50	—	—	—	—	50
H	250	—	—	—	—	250
		320	290	350	340	400

Updating the Plan

Actuals are then compared with this "plan", week by week or even day by day (in a well-run company it will be the latter), with the forward plan being constantly updated in the light of the result.

When this is first done, the weeks into which the jobs have to be allocated (allowing for slippage) to meet delivery promises to customers may well result in an unattainably high number of hours, in total, having to be worked in some weeks, while other weeks show a shortage of productive work available. Allowance needs to be made, too, for "short" months, holidays in July, August and December, bad weather in January, the Easter break etc.

Replanning

The programme will have to be constantly reworked and reworked to produce an ever more feasible pattern, customers delivery dates being rescheduled accordingly (with their consent, or at least knowledge!).

A constantly updated daily or weekly plan will form the focal point for the sales side in quoting and finalising all delivery dates, the sales side informing the customer at once whenever a schedule slips.

Slippage

Note that slippage of one job (perhaps because components are not available in time for the work to start on schedule) will affect other jobs as the plan automatically gets updated day by day or week by week. So it is little good the sales side looking at the plan at the outset, setting delivery dates and then forgetting all about them. They must daily note how scheduled finishing dates are moving backwards or forwards and intervene where necessary, in order to try and maintain customer promises. Recall the 80% curve referred to in the last chapter. Any slippage over estimate in one job will cause slippage in all the other jobs being run at around the same time and in future. So it is a moveable pattern which needs tolerance, but not too much, to steer safely through.

In particular, close liaison is needed between Production and Sales. Reiterating, a simple, reliable method of updating the plan frequently is essential. It should be done at least weekly.

Hours as Measurement of Elapsed Time

Basing this exercise on hours is a useful technique because, besides being a measure of **volume**, the "quantity" side of the contract, it is also, in itself, a measure of **time**. If one tries to do the same thing by reference to the *value* of the contract (collating material costs, labour costs etc., in order to see how the contract is going, as with conventional systems) delays, expense and errors creep in. Inflexibility is created. Constant updates become tedious. They are therefore either not done at all, or not done as regularly as they should be.

Again, measuring the cost or value of a contract does not conveniently lend itself to assessment against readily available bench marks like capacity of the plant or man hours available.

Case History

Going back to the electronics company mentioned in Chapter XII with an output problem. For months management kept promising "next month we *will* get turnover up to £100,000" and being genuinely perplexed when output stuck at £50,000.

Immediately the order book was analysed into hours and allocated to the weeks in which the work was to be done to meet delivery requirements, the reason stood out. The order book comprised at least 20,000 hours of work, assuming all jobs could be finished in no more than the time estimated, to be got out of the door in five months. The company only had 25 employees of which 6 were employed on R & D and 4 more effectively on remedial work.

Assuming a 40 hour week, 4.33 weeks a month, 80% productive efficiency, each employee could contribute around 138 productive hours a month. 15 could work around 2000 hours, *half* what was needed. No wonder the output was only half!

Again when this gap was pointed out all the classic arguments come forward, "we are already losing £15,000 per month. The last thing we can do is to afford to double our workforce". But they could not afford not to. Job value added was at least £12.50 an hour against labour costs of £2.50. 2000 extra hours worked even at an additional cost of £5,000 would generate an extra £25,000 income, turning a £15,000 loss into a £10,000 profit. And with the customers suddenly becoming rather more happy with no longer being let down on delivery dates.

Living Right on Top of the Action

The process can be extended to give you, the MD, you the Sales Director, you the Production Director, you the Finance Director and your staffs, a monthly, weekly or even daily indication of company profitability.

Back-of-the-Envelope Method for Measuring Daily Profitibility

As a matter of routine daily despatches from the Goods Outwards Bay can be listed and the estimated hour content of each job inserted (once you know for certain that you can rely on the estimates). The hours are then multiplied by estimated job value added/hr to give job value added in money terms, which when totalled gives the company's *real income* for the day, the week, the month.

Then from your knowledge of the company's daily cost of operation, which is not going to vary so very much from period to period, you will be able to derive a rough on-the-spot figure for the daily **profit or loss** of the company.

You go home at night elated, . . . or with that sinking feeling in the pit of your stomach.

Planning Production for Profit

You can, of course, get a quick feel for likely profit in any particular week or any particular month (e.g. before finalising the production plan for that week or month) by the same technique, multiplying job hours by respective value addeds and comparing with costs:

Figure 56

PRODUCTION ALTERNATIVES, MONTH ONE

Income

Job	Hrs	VA/Hr	VA£	Hrs	VA/Hr	VA£
	Possibility (1)			Possibility (2)		
A	100	3.75	375	—	—	—
B	40	10.00	400	40	10.00	400
C	50	8.33	417	100	8.33	833
D	400	8.00	3,200	200	8.00	1,600
E	40	7.50	300	40	7.50	300
F	—	—	—	100	12.00	1,200
Total Income	630	7.45Av.	4,692	480	9.02Av.	4,333

Costs

	Hrs.	£/Hr.	VA£	Hrs.	£/Hr.	VA£
Labour						
Productive	630	[3.00]	1,890	480	[2.50]	1,200
Un-Productive	[158]	[3.00]	474	[94]	[2.50]	235
Sub-Total	[788]		2,364	[574]		1,435
Overheads			3,300			3,000
Total Costs	630	9.00Av.	5,664	480	9.23Av.	4,435
Notional Profit(Loss)		(1.55)	(972)		(0.21)	(102)

136

Possibility (1) clearly needs more hours (at overtime rates etc.) and is a weaker "mix" of products earning only £7.45/hr. Possibility (2) produces £359 less value added for 27% less hours and £1,229 less cost. Neither might be acceptable in the particular circumstances of the business, for example, if job A *has* to be got out, but cash flow requires that no week can run at a loss, so a third alternative would need to be constructed. But the system provides the understanding needed to enable you to do so, "on-the-back-of-an-envelope."

Note the above notional "profits" and "losses" won't appear as such in the monthly accounts until the work has actually been got out of the door to the customer. Before then it will remain in stock, with the labour content of stock being valued at no more than say £2.50 (labour cost). Again this might be a consideration in deciding which jobs to run, the cash flow aspect being particularly important.

Quick Payment—Cash Considerations may be paramount

The cash needs of the company may demand that you get work out of the door that attracts quick payment (say one month) rather than prolonged payment (three to six months), even though margin and value added are lower than you would like for a good result. But if this is the case, plan accordingly in your estimates. Everyone is then prepared for the profit hiccup, knows about it in advance and can view events accordingly.

Predictability

The test of whether, for instance, a Banker can trust a company lies in its *predictability*. The more predictable it is (good or bad) the more he knows that management understand what they are doing and firmly have the levers of control in their hands.

Financial Support

Take again the example of the company that expected to get £100,000 per month out of the door and only achieved £50,000. Management genuinely believed they would succeed, which only made matters worse! An outsider knows they have not got a proper grip, a proper understanding. That makes them perhaps unacceptably accident-prone. So you as a Banker tend to distrust them and become cautious about entrusting too much of your (or rather your Depositors') money to them.

How different is the "feel" of a company that knows, down to the last nut and bolt, what they are doing. You can trust their estimates, however unnerving. Such a company is far more likely to get support it needs, even, indeed particularly, through a bad period.

Professionalism

It is hoped the techniques set out in this book will enable you to become fully predictable and sure-footed in running your company. It is what is meant, of course, by professionalism. As hopefully this book has shown, the techniques are far from just common sense and learning on the job is *not* to be recommended.

Chapter XV

IMPROVING GROSS MARGINS

A final word about margins. The margin problem, wherein the true "bite" of a business lies, can be summed up as follows:

Suppose, firstly, you are locked in at present prices. Margins can only be improved by:

(1) Reducing direct sales cost content (commissions, freight, discounts etc.)
(2) Reducing material content (better buying, changed specification, redesign etc.)
(3) reducing labour content (improved production methods, redesign of product etc.).

The issues are conceptually set out in Figure 57.

Low Margins

Suppose existing margins are only 12% (first column). Just *one* percentage point (of turnover) knocked off each of the three heads takes margin from 12% to 15%, improving real income by one quarter (12% to 15%). *So very small reductions in direct cost improvements can have a very big impact and are fully worth going for relentlessly.*

Just 4% off each of the three main heads doubles real income to 24% (second column).

Medium Margins

A further 8% off labour (making 12% in all) and materials (ditto) and 4% off direct sales costs (making 8% in all) lifts gross margin to 44% (third column) where it is beginning to get into the "healthy" range, producing nearly *four times* more real income than it did at the start, for no change in sales price.

So be bold. And the engineers and scientists can have a field day here in:

(1) redesigning the product
(2) redesigning the production process

to achieve these ends.

Combining Margin Cost Improvement with Price Improvement

But it is rare for price to be absolutely unchangeable. Combine cost savings (or increases) with sale price adjustments (up or down) and whole new worlds open up, as schematically represented in Figure 58.

Over-Engineered Products

One often hears of a product being "over-engineered". The materials that go into it are unnecessarily durable for the function it has to perform and are therefore unnecessarily costly, both in terms of material content itself and in the number of hours, and therefore cost, taken to manufacture. Technical specification could be met with simpler design.

Reducing Material Content

One of Britain's leading high-performance car companies at one time mounted a trial whereby metal was progressively pared off all the components of the car, including the engine block, until failure occurred. They were surprised how far they could go. They found it was then possible to design not only a cheaper car but a lighter and therefore faster car; and a more economical car. Furthermore with more space available, they could also design stylistically a more attractive car. Such was customer satisfaction, they found they could even charge a premium! So the margin was expanded from *both* ends, represented by moving from price range A first column to price range B second column.

Charge for the Engineering

Maybe the customer *does* need the extra engineering. If so, charge for it moving from price range A first column to price ranges B or C first column. Incidentally product design should always start with finding out precisely and painstakingly what the customer wants, at what price, and working back to the product. Not vice versa. Fords are a distinguished example.

Reliability

This is particularly important where the **customer,** for the sake of his own business, **wants reliability**. Equipment breakdown can cost a literal fortune in lost business. A halted production line is failing to generate £10, £20, £50 value added per hour whilst "down", as indicated in the last chapter. The customer will set the cost of the reliability you offer against that risk. *Your price should be fixed in relation to the benefit to him, not your own costs.* By definition, the more reliable your product and the more reliable your delivery, the more you will help your customer to avoid disruption to *his* production process. The more he should therefore be prepared to pay you.

Figure 57

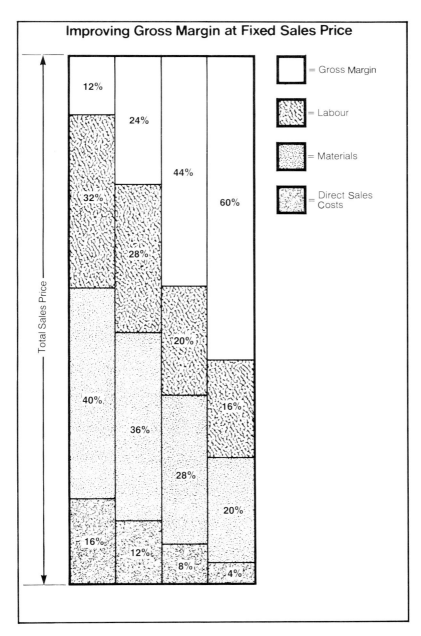

141

Engineering Design

So once you, the engineer, understand not only your own business but your customer's, you can begin to apply your own specialist skills to design to your and your customer's value added needs, which is where the key benefit to the company will lie, but which only *you* are able to supply.

An Example

Returning to the Plastics Company mentioned in Chapter IV. So weak were market conditions when the 73/74 recession hit that there seemed little prospect of getting prices up. However the customers, the food manufacturers, found *their* sales slipping in the same recession. The company redesigned the product range, installing co-extrusion equipment to put a bright white gloss onto the outside of the containers and re-equipped the plant with 8-colour printers, replacing the old 2 to 4 colour.

It cost a fortune, but the company was first into the market with a container range that induced the housewife to reach for X's products rather than Y's on the supermarket shelves, just at the very moment the food manufacturers most needed sales.

Naturally the food manufacturers bought the new range. The fact it cost an extra pound or two per thousand containers was neither here nor there. But for a plant with a production capacity of 2 million containers a day, the extra unit value, however small, and the considerably higher volume of containers it was possible to sell, brought a doubled benefit. Skilled design and engineering, conducted with the sharpest possible instinct into the real and urgent needs of the business, shot the company into profit, at the height of the recession.

Styling

Here we come to the question of aesthetics. A product that is pleasing to the eye, well proportioned, skilfully made and blended with materials of the right texture, colour, shape and styling, will always outsell the dull product, even for surprisingly routine equipment used in unaesthetic surroundings like a work-shop or a laboratory. Good styling inspires confidence. "A good deal of thought and effort has gone into the styling, so it must have gone into the product itself. Here is a company who obviously cares and pays painstaking attention to detail. Clearly they must be worth dealing with". So the thinking will go.

If, in restyling a product you can also make it cheaper in material and labour content, again you will be expanding the margin from both ends. As has already been shown, even a few percentage points here and a few percentage points there can have a quite disproportionate effect.

Figure 58

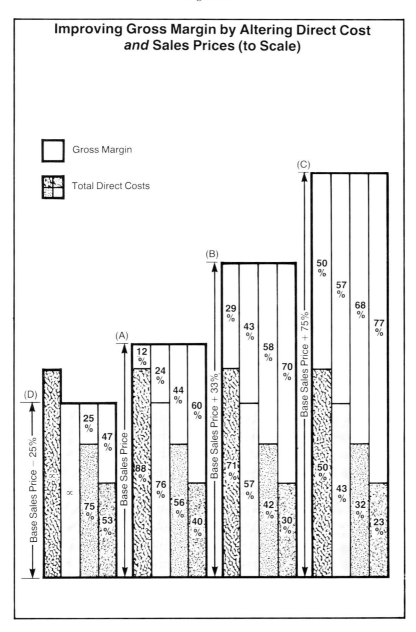

Decreasing Cost whilst Increasing Appeal
So, more frequently than is often thought, there may be scope for both making a product cheaper *and* heightening its appeal to the customer by building in reliability, styling and so on.

Deliberately Cheapening a Product
That leaves a further alternative, If the customer, in reality, does not *want* all the engineering sophistication and durability you have built into the product, price range A first column, and would be happy with something more simple and straightforward but at a lower price, maybe you can widen margin that way (third and fourth columns dropping to price range D).

Another Example
A UK company making standard-range saucepans found an influx of cheap imports suddenly destroying sales in the shops just as overseas markets were drying up in the recession. Up went the cry of dumping. The competing saucepans were priced at a massive £1 lower (20%) than their own. The company plummeted into loss.

Fortunately a sense of self-help prevailed, a bright engineer was brought in to study the problem. He merely placed the two saucepans side by side and noticed the following. The foreign product:

(1) was 1cm shorter,
(2) had no lip,
(3) was made of fractionally thinner material,
(4) the join between the sides and base was slightly rounded, rather than square.

Costed up, the first three represented 14p saving in raw material costs; and the different method of manufacture implied by (4) could be made to result in 2 minutes saving in production time (worth say 12p).

26p scaled up through the gross profit percentage (50% on prime cost=33% gross margin), the wholesaler's margin (50%) and the retailer's mark up (100%) produced a reduction in retail price of 117p! Without the additional transport costs from the Far East, the competition could be met head-on and defeated. And it was. Again it will be noted how small the changes at the cost-of-sales end can often be to produce quite disproportionately large changes at the sales-price end.

British Engineering Skill
Technically, we are still the most marvellously ingenious and inventive of nations. When we fail in business, where we ought to be so pre-eminent, we do so because we don't apply the related skills needed to make business work. What greater challenge is there to the engineers and scientists who read this book?

With notable exceptions like British Leyland or Rolls Royce, engineers for the most part tend to feel outsiders where British industry is concerned. Hopefully this book can help to accelerate bringing about the necessary changes in feeling and attitude by making you the Engineer much more willing to enter the business scene and you the Industrialist much more willing to have him, and more willing to bring him right into the centre of your operations, where his role, as hopefully has been shown, is crucial, reaching right down into the very fundamentals of the business itself.

The American Scene
A fascinating report on the American Venture Capital scene, prepared in mid 1982 for Congress by the US General Accounting Office, follows the history of 1,332 companies financed by American venture capital in the 1970s.

Type of Company
Listing the type of company supported, by nature of its product or service, the report notes:
> "54% of the ventures and 61% of the capital went to companies offering productivity-related products, systems and services. Of the 72 real high-flyers that went public in that time, *all* related to such activities."

Type of Product
"Productivity-related" of course means products or services designed to help customers to improve their own value added, their own gross margins. The radio-active scanning equipment that enabled the plastics company to make thinner sheets saved 4% of raw material cost. The co-extrusion equipment and eight colour printers for the same company enabled a better appearance to be given to the outside of the container. Computer-Aided-Design equipment, quoted as an example at the end of the US report, enabled one aerospace equipment company to lay out a cockpit instrument panel in two hours against the one week it took when previously done manually. Another company saved 28,000 hours design work a year (35%). This resulted not so much in a reduced workforce *but in accelerated product development. This enabled the customer to keep further ahead of the competition in the market-place.*

The Financial Side
In the ten years from 1969 to 1979, the CAD's company's sales grew from $51,000 to $131.5m; after-tax profits rose to $12.9m.

$33m was invested in research and development. Asset value grew to $40.6m.

800 systems were sold to 500 companies. 2,500 jobs were created, a figure that has since risen to 4,000.

$18m was paid in taxes. Additionally by 1979 payroll taxes were running at $2m pa and exports at $40m.

The People Behind the Company

The CAD company started with just two people, a bright *engineer* and bright *manager* getting together. As the report comments:

> "The idea was conceived while both founders were working for a large, technologically oriented firm, after extensive discussion with a group of engineering *professors*."

The Intimate Fusion between Academics, Engineers and Businessmen

Here we have that crucial fusion of businessmen, engineers and academics, brought together in the most intimate and fundamental way, to make business WORK. It must be the mainspring that makes any successful business tick, particularly in the high technology field. Note how the product, while itself carrying a very good margin, was taken up widely by no less than 500 companies because it helped them also to dramatically increase their margins. This crucially depended on the engineers having a very intimate understanding not just of how their own, but how other people's, businesses worked. The deepest understanding of what is really meant, for instance, by the value added concept.

What the Founders Got Out of it

The report goes on:

> "As of March 1980" (as sales headed for $200m) "the founders still owned 22% of the outstanding stock".

Capitalising the Company on a multiple of, say, 30 times post-tax profits, this made them, the Originators, in just over a decade, worth a modest $85m.

The UK Equivalent

There have been equally successful UK companies. Oxford Instruments for instance began in 1959 when Martin Wood, an engineer working at the Clarendon Laboratory, started making high-field magnets for University research.

The Product

The company came to specialise in the making of super-conducting magnets. Super-conducting magnets have to be cooled by jackets of liquid helium and liquid nitrogen, to Absolute zero, minus 273 degrees

Centigrade. In the early days if anything went wrong, for whatever reason, and the magnets suddenly heated up, they instantly vaporised the helium and nitrogen jackets, producing a very passable imitation of a Roman Candle.

Medical Use

Technical problems such as this had to be overcome to produce, two decades and many excitements later, completely safe, high-field, super-conducting magnets for scientific, industrial and medical use.

This took the Company into the Nuclear Magnetic Resonance field, or "NMR" as it is called. Atomic nuclei can be made to behave in very high magnetic fields rather like minute radio transmitters. This led Oxford Instruments to play an active role in pioneering the development of the NMR body scanner. These machines produce detailed images of sections of the human body without any of the dangers associated with X-rays. Oxford Instruments is now a world leader in providing magnets for such equipment.

Financial Performance

Sales built up steadily through the 60s and 70s. In 1979 the advent of NMR body-scanners began a period of more rapid growth. In 1979 sales were £5.5m, in 1980 £7.5m, 1981 £11.5m, 1982 £16.5m, 1983 £26.0m, which may still be just a start. Trading profits have climbed from £0.8m in 1979 to £3.4m in 1983 with £5.7m in prospect for 1984. Over 950 people are employed and 70% of sales go for export. When the shares were floated in October 1983 they were 9.2 times oversubscribed and went off at £2.85 per share, valuing the company at £126.4m and the stake of Martin Wood and his family at £31.4m.

The Paramount Importance of People

The later success of Oxford Instruments has depended substantially on the timely arrival of managers who enjoy the pioneering spirit of a small company but bring professionalism and wider experience to bear. All of them are now shareholders.

Where the Founder's Business Skill came from

Martin Wood himself had to learn what he could about business as the operation built up around him.

Oxford Instruments has been an outstanding success. However Martin Wood would be the first to admit that mistakes were made on the way which at one time or another seriously held back, or even actually endangered, the whole operation; mistakes made in the utmost good faith, but which might not have been made had **his own business knowledge** been surer from the outset. **However there was nowhere to turn to acquire it. He just had to** pick up what he could on the way. Not a course to be recommended in a highly volatile new business operation, trying to penetrate new markets with new products and new management teams.

Other companies have not been so fortunate. They have failed despite the brilliance of their products, despite the technical excellence and dedication of their mangement teams, just because of this lack of business knowledge, this absence of general business awareness, which seems a feature of the UK scene. The very success of Oxford Instruments as one of a comparative handful that did survive, may be living proof of just how much the poorer the nation is as a result.

Our research laboratories are literally filled to the eaves with good ideas just as excellent as the super-conducting magnet or Nuclear Magnetic Resonance. If this had been America or Japan, dozens if not hundreds of new companies like Oxford Instruments would have been spawned over the past two decades and would have seen their way through to success, perhaps in a considerably shorter time-scale than the 24 years it took Oxford Instruments.

However, Oxford Instruments is also living proof of what *can* be done once we put our minds to it and how great the potential *really is* in the UK.

Japanese Competition

In the light of all that has been said about the way engineers could and should be putting their talents to work at the very heart of British industry, it begins to become apparent why the Japanese are so successful. Consider the following facts. D. F. G. Marshall, Scientific Counsellor of the British Embassy in Tokyo gave a talk in 1982 in which he said:

> "A startling fact is that Japan, with just twice the population of the UK, in 1978 awarded 71,167 degrees in engineering compared with 6,897 in the UK."

> Another startling fact is that "Japan employs more scientists and engineers in Research and Development than France, Germany and the UK combined".

> The USA by comparison awarded 12,338 degrees in electrical engineering, electronics and communications, four times the UK number but one fifth of the Japanese.

> Out of 10,000 Americans 20 are lawyers, 40 are accountants and 70 engineers. In Japan one is a lawyer, three are accountants and 400 are engineers.

The last feature may mean, incidentally, that with no formalised accountancy profession to guide them, Japanese businessmen may have had to evolve their own financial and business techniques from scratch. This will have been done, essentially, by engineers, to produce techniques that are now highly relevant and beneficial to Japanese business.

In countries like Britain and America the professions have developed separately from business and quite a wide gulf now seems to exist between what is provided (the "static") and what is needed (the "dynamic"). This may explain why, for instance, rather too little of what is set out in this book seems to appear anywhere in formalised professional, accounting, banking or business school training.

Japanese Engineer-Businessmen

These engineers in a sense *are* the businessmen. The success of Japanese economic strength must lie in the fact that the two disciplines have come to be inseparably merged as one. That in turn gives rise to the challenges, the fascinations, the excitements that attract so many gifted students into engineering in the first place.

Why not the UK?

However, as this book has attempted to show, there is *no* reason why, the UK cannot be equally successful. The Japanese are said to devote 7% of their time to producing original ideas, 93% to "commercialising" the ideas of others. It must be the other way round in the UK. Given the stimulus, there is *no* reason why this cannot be changed.

Employment

Unemployment levels in the leading industrial nations in late 1982 were as follows:

Figure 59

UNEMPLOYMENT AS PERCENTAGE OF WORKING POPULATION	
UK	13.4%
America	10.2%
France	8.3%
Germany	7.2%
Japan	2.5%

If the theory can be advanced that in any country there must be a relationship between the strength of the economy and the strength of the business sector, between the degree of business understanding and level of unemployment, then the figures speak for themselves.

Given all the facts, the only surprise perhaps is that the UK is not even further down the league!

Chapter XVI

COMPANY DOCTORING

We are now in a position to bring together the profit improvement exercises and cash flow measures into a unified means of helping companies to survive and succeed.

We saw in Chapter V and elsewhere how losses could be stemmed by hardening margins and allowing volume to fall back.

Reduced turnover of course also reduces the working capital requirement, since stock and debtor levels in a well-run company can be pegged back *pro rata*.

Let's see how the cash side of this radical-scale-back exercise works. The following three very different levels of operation produce the same £5,000 gross margin, to "cover" a £5,000 per month overhead:

Figure 60

"COMPANY DOCTORING"

	%	%	%
Gross Margin	10	25	50
Breakeven Sales	50	20	10
Labour (say)	15	5	1.5
Materials (say)	30	10	3.5
Cost of Sales	45	15	5.0
Gross Margin	5	5	5.0
Working Capital			
Debtors (2 months)	100	40	20
R.M. (6 weeks)	45	15	5
W.I.P. (1 month)	45	15	5
F.G. (1 month)	45	15	5
	235	85	35
Creditors			
(3 months purchases)	(90)	(30)	(10)
Capital Need	145	55	25

The first objective is to get turnover to drop like a stone. So margins are forced up, represented by the breakeven point coming down from £50,000 per month to £20,000, to £10,000. As turnover plummets, given good control, large sums can be shaken out of stocks and debtors; £150,000 (from £235,000 to £85,000) in dropping monthly turnover from £50,000 to £20,000, and a further £50,000 in dropping to £10,000.

Use of Cash to Effect Restructuring

This provides cash:

(1) To reduce creditors
(2) To finance however many months losses occur before the company begins to come into profit
(3) To refurbish, overhaul and upgrade plant and equipment, rebuild and modernise the production line, etc.
(4) To embark on an extensive R & D and product redesign programme.

Don't Leave the Exercise too Late

The exercise obviously needs to be started in good time, before creditors get too high and absorb the bulk of the cash that would otherwise become available for purposes (2) (3) and (4). If all goes well by the time the cash runs out, the company should be fully re-equipped and modernised with upgraded products, improved margins and well able to live profitably at whatever new level the market settles.

Overheads

Note in all of this we have not once discussed overheads, the conventional way of cutting-back. Possibly overheads should be *increased* rather than decreased, in upgraded staff, harder marketing, accelerated R & D, to achieve improved "quality". Conversely a business, as in this example, with 5 times less turnover and 9 times less volume (compare cost of sales) should not need the same "volume" overhead. So cuts *can* be made. But it is likely to be rather different from the typical cheese-paring exercise of simply shedding people and premises, which may leave a company leaner and weaker rather than leaner and fitter. New strength must be created from the old, not an operation dismantled piece-meal as markets collapse all around.

Incidentally, the latest UK recession is often spoken of, admiringly, as having somehow brought about a sharp improvement in "productivity", as workforces are laid off throughout the country.

Stronger Companies?

Unfortunately only in certain cases will this be true, only where companies in fact have the necessary business understanding to make use of the scale-back to bring about qualitative changes of the kind mentioned in this book. Otherwise, as soon as the recession eases the companies may go back to the same congested ways as before, remaining relatively small and unable to meet market need as demand expands, to the benefit of importers and the detriment of the economy as imports flood in.

A further example, dealing now with a very young company in its formative years:

Figure 61

SCALING BACK (MONTHLY RESULTS)

£'000

	(1)	(2)	(3)	(4)	(5)
Overhead say	10	5	5		
Gross Margin Percentage	40%	40%	75%		
Breakeven	25	13	7		
Actual Sales	5	5	4		
Profit/(Loss)	(8)	(3)	(2)	(1)	b/e

Suppose the company starts with funding of say £50,000. At a loss of £8,000 per month it will run out of money after about 6 months.

If the loss can be halved, remaining life time will be doubled. And so on.

Large Companies will not Normally Trade with Small Companies Initially

As a general rule, larger companies will not trade with young and small companies, however good their products or services, until the small company has been in existence for at least 3 years—to prove its survivability. Most companies, if they are going to fail will do so within the first 3 years. They do not come out of the "death valley" curve illustrated in Figure 26, but go straight on down. . . .

Most large companies will be using the small companies as sub-contractors, effectively plugging them into their own production lines. They will therefore be at the greatest pains to ensure that no disruption of supply occurs. So the sub-contractor's survival has not only got to be self-evident and durable, but he has to be adequately funded to handle the business. Above all cash must not become exhausted before he gets safely through death valley, on which the big company will "credit check".

Very common is the situation where for 2 or 3 years a large customer may seem genuinely interested in the product and may even place a trial order just to keep his interest warm, but the promised orders never really materialise or do not do so until the operation has reached "durability" point, which could even be up to 5 years.

No explanation of this will be available! Any company who gears up to handle the expected volume (Column 1), is thus likely to run out of finance long before sufficient orders come in.

Extending the Life of a Company

So the first move is to come to terms with the very much longer run-in time likely (3 to 5 years, rather than 3 to 5 months) and to cut the operation right back (Column 2), which will more than double life to around 18 months; but this is still far too short.

The next step therefore is to force up margins somehow. Column 3 represents a forcing up of price to the equivalent of 75% GM.

The extraordinary feature again is that although sales are running at only £5,000 per month, the company can afford to lose up to ⅔rds of its volume and still be better off:

Figure 62

EFFECT OF PRICE INCREASE

	Before	After
Sales	5,000	4,000
Cost of Sales	3,000	1,000
Gross Margin	2,000	3,000
Improvement		1,000

Monthly losses drop to £2,000, giving around 2 years life.

Still not enough of course. If sales can be built back to just over £5,000 at the higher margins, losses will halve to £1,000 per month, giving 4 years life (Column 4 of Figure 61).

Of course the ultimate "first-base" objective is to get as quickly as possible to breakeven, after recouping all R & D, etc. The company is then in a notional "parking orbit". It can safely stay there for as long as it takes to get volume business on-stream. These are good tactics in the early days and, if they can be achieved, will give the maximum chance of long term survival and success.

Chapter XVII

CONTROL AND EVALUATION OF STOCK

Stock Figures need to be Accurate for Margin Purposes

Control and evaluation of stock is a somewhat tricky subject. The stock figure does of course need to be accurate for the purposes of calculating gross margin, see Appendix, page 177, lines (12) and (23). The whole thrust of a company's operation depends on it. So a few tips on how you can satisfy yourself that it *is* accurate may be useful. It may not be physically possible to count stock every month, if only on grounds of the time-scale involved.

The principle behind the method used to analyse sales in Chapter XI is to keep the procedure as simple as possible. This is done by focussing on material content and labour hours *only*.

Stock and Job Records kept Simple

Given this starting point all Stock and Work-in-Progress records can be kept very simple with a "Job Card" for each job recording only the build-up of *material* and *hours* as work moves through the factory or construction site until it is completed and despatched. (Where a job is despatched in parts or stages "completion" constitutes the state of the whole contract after completion of the *final* stage or final despatch and after inclusion of all labour and material costs throughout the life of the contract.)

"Completed" Jobs

The completed "Job" or "Contract" cards then provide the information needed to prepare the sales analysis. Labour *costs* are found by multiplying the *hours* column by an *average rate per hour*, found as follows.

Total payroll costs per productive hour (including employers' pension and NHI contributions, etc.) will be known globally from monitoring the monthly payroll and total productive hours worked. The average rate per hour is found by dividing one by the other. It will of course change from month to month, but not by a large amount. It is the *rate per hour* that is being measured. A broad average taken for total payroll costs per productive hour for the period covering the life of the contract should then suffice, giving more than acceptable accuracy.

Distinction between Sales and Production

In any one month work may be done on a job that was either "in-progress" at the start of the month i.e. had already had work done on it in previous months, but is not yet complete; or on new jobs that may not be completed and despatched for some months yet.

So a very careful distinction needs to be drawn between production and sales. For instance, unless all work done in the month is despatched in the month, the *total labour cost in sales* (11) will not "reconcile" with *total payroll costs for the month* (6), for the purposes of checking the accuracy of the analysis given in Chapter XI.

Similarly on the materials side, *materials delivered* to the company in the month (5) is unlikely to be the same figure as material content *used* in production.

Raw Material Stock *v* Work-in-Progress

As an added complication *materials delivered* to the company (5) may or may not go straight into *work-in-progress* (33) on the factory floor. Part may go into *raw material stock* (32) to be booked out later to production as it is used.

"Ins" and "Outs"

The principle behind "reconciling" Stock or Work-in-Progress is reasonably straightforward. Add to opening stock or work-in-progress the material and wage costs incurred in the month and deduct the material and wage content of work despatched ("sales"). What is left, if all items have been successfully traced, will be the closing stock or work-in-progress.

Thus for raw material stock:

Figure 63

RAW MATERIAL STOCK

	£'000
Opening stock	30
Add: Deliveries by supplier	27
Less: Issued to production	(22)
Closing stock	35

Tracing all Items

If this does not produce a closing stock figure that agrees with the *physical* stock on the premises at the end of the month you *must* trace back all transactions until it does. *Otherwise cost is being incurred that is not being identified and will not be known about.*

Many things can of course go wrong.

Firstly, issues to production may not have been properly recorded. You want to keep your procedures as simple as possible, but they may be too approximate.

Secondly, you may be short-delivered, the supplier invoices you for more goods than you have actually received, double-invoices, or charges more than he has previously quoted.

A supplier should not therefore be paid until his invoice has been matched with:

(1) Proof of delivery (i.e. the supplier's "Advice Note" signed by your own staff; or your own "Goods Inwards Note");

(2) Confirmation of price (against the Quote your supplier will have provided you with before you ordered from him).

Thirdly, of course, there may be pilferage, on or off the premises.

Fourthly, there may be errors in the stock-take itself.

Check, Check, Check, until Accuracy is Routine

As a general rule, however difficult and although it will involve extra work initially, you should endeavour to count all your stock every month until the month-end "reconciliation" in Figure 63 is tying up regularly without any trouble. Remember it is a cost identification exercise. You *must* nail down:

(1) That you are not paying for anything you do not use;

(2) That you are showing the full cost of everything you do use.

Work-in-Progress "Stock"

A similar exercise is possible on work-in-progress. Firstly, dealing with the materials aspect, the *material content* of all the "uncompleted" job cards at the start of the month and all uncompleted cards at the end of the month is totalled to give opening and closing stock, then reconciled, Figure 64. The same can be done on the labour side, Figure 65. This gives an overall picture as shown in Figure 66.

Figure 64

MATERIAL CONTENT OF WORK-IN-PROGRESS

	£'000
Opening Work-in-Progress	40
Add: Material used:	
Issues from Raw Material stock (as in Figure 63)	22
Delivered by supplier direct to production	13
Deduct: Material content of sales	(28)
Closing Work-in-Progress	47

Figure 65

LABOUR CONTENT OF WORK-IN-PROGRESS

	Productive Hours
Opening Work-in-Progress	14,000
Worked in Month	6,000
(In sales)	(4,800)
Closing Work-in-Progress	15,200

Figure 66

WORK-IN-PROGRESS RECONCILIATION

		Materials	Labour Hrs.	Labour £'000 (@ say £2.50hr.)	Total £'000
		£'000			
Opening Stock:	R.M.	30 ⎫	14,000	35	105
	W.I.P.	40 ⎭			
Material Deliveries in month		40	—	—	40
Wages in Month		—	6,000	15	15
*(In Sales in Month)		(28)	(4,800)	(12)	(40)
Closing Stock:	R.M.	35 ⎫	15,200	38	120
	W.I.P.	47 ⎭			

*These cost of sales figures should of course fully agree with the totals shown in the monthly sales analysis.

Transfers between raw materials stock and work-in-progress have been netted-out to give the overall reconciliation, which ensures:

(1) *All* material costs;

(2) *All* payroll costs,

are accounted for.

"Slippage"

Any "wastage", unaccounted-for materials or non-productive labour, should be specifically identified "below-the-line" as done for instance in Figure 45 and included in cost of sales in the monthly accounts. The prompt regular and accurate identification of *all* such items, with immediate action being taken to limit them to a minimum, can make all the difference between success and failure.

Curtailment of "wastage" also enables you effectively to run a higher-margin company, in turn enabling you to get more potential from "trading" in the market place, in terms of precise pricing.

Close Books Quickly

Note one significant point in passing. If in order to get accounts out quickly you have to close-the-books before, for example, all suppliers invoices are available, it does not matter too much. All that happens is that material deliveries (5), i.e. purchases, are lower by the amount left out. But raw material stocks (10) are equally affected. The two cancel out and the cost of sales figure (11) is unaffected. The only essential is that *by the time a job is "completed" the full material content must be accounted for*, because that content *will* influence the gross margin and value added shown in cost of sales (11) in the accounts.

Given this system, production can be analysed in just the same way as sales, and if wanted work-in-progress can be scheduled in the same way.

Referring back to Figure 20 in Chapter VIII, it will be seen that the cost of sales side of the profit and loss account is derivable directly from the method just given, viz.:

Figure 67

COST OF SALES	
Opening stock	105
Purchases	40
Labour	15
(Closing Stock)	(120)
Cost of Sales	40

"cost of sales" merely being another way of expressing the material and labour content of sales, thus enabling gross margin and value added to be arrived at.

Overhead Element in Stock

Raw material stock, work-in-progress and finished goods stock in the discussion so far consist of labour and material costs *only*.

Some companies make life unnecessarily complicated for themselves—and unnecessarily inaccurate, particularly as regards derivation of accurate gross margins (see below)—by including an "overhead element" in stock.

The rationale for doing so is that if a contract takes 6 months to get out of the door, at the end of that period, on completion, overheads will be "recovered" in full (hopefully!) in the sales price.

So every month the appropriate portion of overhead (usually expressed as a multiple of basic labour cost, or basic labour rate per hour, say 2½ times) is taken out of the total overhead shown in the accounts (17) and added to stock (10); just as in Figure 13 in Chapter VI where £5,000 or £3,000 per month was "capitalised".

The Method can Introduce Big Inaccuracies into the Calculation of Breakeven, etc.

This *cannot* in any way affect Cash Flow, as discussed in Chapter VIII. It is purely a book entry. But it does have a very big impact on the apparent dynamic of the company, for:

(1) depending on treatment, it can improve the apparent gross margin (12) and apparent gross margin percentage (23);
(2) it can lower the apparent overhead (17);
(3) it can thus substantially lower the apparent breakeven point (24) and therefore,
(4) much increase apparent profitability (18).

Exactly what "overhead" element to syphon out in this way can effectively be made a matter of choice. Accountants must adhere to certain carefully laid-down guidelines for the purpose of preparing annual audited accounts, but it is possible in *management* accounts to show as much apparent profit or loss as you wish, at least for a time!

Cash Black Hole

A company can then sail on, blithely unaware anything is amiss, until a sudden "cash black hole" opens beneath it, swallowing it up.

This in part is the background to the very scenario portrayed in Chapter VI.

(Figure 13 is appropriately numbered!) It is the company equivalent of an Exocet attack with the danger possibly being wholly unforseen until a short while before it strikes. By then it may be far too late to do anything about it.

As an example let's "tamper" with a typical profit and loss account as follows:

Figure 68

EFFECT OF INCLUDING AN ARBITARY OVERHEAD ELEMENT IN STOCK

Overhead Element	£'000 None	£'000 15	£'000 30
Sales	45	45	45
Opening Stock (Direct cost content)	105	105	105
Materials	40	40	40
Labour	15	15	15
Less: Closing Stock	(120)	(130)	(140)
Apparent **Cost of Sales**	40	30	20
Apparent **Gross Margin**	5	15	25
Opening Stock (Overhead content)	—	—	—
Gross Overheads	12	12	12
Less: Closing Stock	—	(5)	(10)
Apparent **Overheads**	12	7	2
Apparent **Profit/(Loss)**	(7)	8	23
Apparent **Gross Margin Percentage**	11%	33%	56%
Apparent **Breakeven Point**	108	21	4

Rather daunting isn't it? There is a factor that operates the other way. A brought-forward error in opening stock will have no effect on cost of sales to the extent that same error is included in closing stock. This will *not* be true of course if the work in question is despatched in the month instead of being carried forward in stock into later months. Given that stock figures appearing in most sets of accounts may, in reality, be no more than broad guesstimates anyway, however "scientific" their apparent preparation, it can be a hit and miss affair. Every £1 error in stocks creates a £1 error in profit and therefore in management's perception of the business. Unfortunately, similar errors can even creep into audited accounts especially where stock is "as valued by management".

Management Figures should Provide Accurate Guidance

The purpose of providing monthly management figures is of course to provide accurate guidance on what is happening in the business and what needs to be done to rectify any deficiencies. Figures that mislead, however unintentionally, will invariably lead the company in the wrong direction, by for instance, not prompting management to raise prices when there is an urgent need to do so with perhaps serious or even fatal consequences. Many otherwise fine companies have gone under, often "out of the blue", to the total perplexity of their management teams for this very reason.

The adjustment may be intentional: a management team may want to show acceptable results, however bad the reality. Or it can be unintentional, perhaps arising from use of guessed rather than measured stock figures. Or it may consist of just general errors creeping into stock figures, particularly if production slippages are allowed to remain in stock, rather than deliberately being extracted into cost of sales.

The possibilities of error can be avoided by ensuring that the work-in-progress figures are precisely arrived at from correctly compiled job cards, along the lines of the discussion at the start of this chapter and by ensuring in particular that *no* production slippages, mark-ups or overhead elements of any kind are included in stock.

Besides in itself creating preciseness, for instance for the purpose of measuring margins, the method of recording of all stock by labour and materials, only, very much simplifies the task of record-keeping and preparing accounts in general, particularly if computers are available.

Exclude All Overhead Element

This goes to the heart of why no overhead element of any kind is included in work-in-progress or finished goods stock in the form of management accounts, budgets and cash flows used in this book.

There is in fact a slot in the P&L format given at Appendix (19) and (20) for an overhead element, for companies who insist on including it, but it is shown "below the line" so as not to affect calculation of gross margin, overheads, breakeven point, etc. Note again it is a non-cash item so cannot affect cash flow.

Other Conventional Accounting Dangers

A similar, equally misleading, distortion can sometimes occur in conventional management accounts on account of:

   (1) Material purchases (5),

   (2) Labour costs (6),

   (3) Overheads (13),

where what is shown is not, as it appears to be, the actual costs *incurred* in the month, which is the vital aspect to monitor for control purposes *because that is the true measure of cash going out of the business*. Some other figure occurs, like the labour and material *content of sales*, or *used in production*, which can be something rather different.

Alarm!

Traditional accounts are structured for a different purpose. But you should be aware of this trap with conventional formats and change as soon as you can to the safer, more accurate and more alarming layouts discussed in this book.

More alarming? Of course. You cannot dupe yourself (however innocently) about what is *really* happening in your company. Fail to get product out of the door and it shows up as a thumping great loss, which is the way it should be. It delineates the real cash world.

The world by which you live.

Or die.

Chapter XVIII

CONCLUSIONS

The full flavour of this book, in helping you to get the right answers in business, will almost certainly not emerge until you have had a chance to put the techniques into practice in a real life business situation and have experienced the results for yourself, in a very direct way. The book may also need to be read and re-read two or three times in order to get a full grasp of the way in which the various factors inter-relate.

However, in summary, it is cash flow, not profit, that really matters in a business. Look after cash flow and the profit will look after itself. Gross margin, not sales, constitutes the *real* income of a business.

It is often easier to close a loss-making gap by reducing breakeven point, which is found by dividing fixed cost by gross margin percentage, than by increasing sales. It is undeniably the safer and more certain course of action, particularly in rapidly changing and unpredictable market conditions.

The Engineers have an absolutely key role to play in building gross margin into the product, whilst keeping a beady eye on breakeven to ensure they are not unacceptably loading up overheads with higher depreciation, interest and other fixed costs. The object is to *reduce* overall breakeven point, not increase it.

Management's business perception and the form and promptness of monthly management information seem to exactly mirror each other. Very well run companies get out key data weekly, not more than 2 days after the end of each week.

Most companies taking longer than about 21 days to produce such data, or producing it less frequently than monthly, can't be considered "well managed". Management who *really* understand business would not dare to wait as long. They would know that too much can go wrong too quickly. The list of how many U.K. companies can be considered really "well run" should be fairly easily assessable on this test.

Any shortcomings are almost certainly due to our cultural heritage and past habits of (quite wrongly) treating business as a second grade operation, needing no particular skills, no particular formalised professionalism. As a result those who want to learn the skills have few places to turn.

This is in stark contrast to our overseas competitors. The rougher the time they are giving our industries and our economy, the greater their own professionalism, knowledge and understanding must be.

If only we could put this right, we have skills that others have not. We are a particularly inventive nation. Our Scientists, our Engineers, our Academics, our Lawyers, our Accountants, our Bankers, our Civil Servants, by the very standards of their own professions and occupations are pre-eminent.

If only the necessary Business Knowledge could now be grafted on, throughout this scene, the effects could be startling.

None of this is to deny that some very fine, very well run, British businesses exist. Their very successes are proof of what could be achieved if only this fusion of knowledge and technical ability could quickly come to be made general throughout the scene.

This book is an attempt to pioneer the way.

Now it's up to YOU.

NOTE

A complete, fully-integrated, book-keeping system should shortly be available capable of producing the formats set out in this book (including the appendix) on a real-time, day-by-day, week-by-week and month-by-month basis.

Details are available from Osmosis Publications

APPENDIX

DETAILED CASH FLOW FORMATS

APPENDIX
CASH FLOW FORECASTING

The motto over the main entrance of one of America's leading companies is said to read: "Our job isn't making steel, it's making money".

Companies with a strong sense of commercial know-how will make money out of even the most indifferent products. They apply the Barrow Boy technique: "If goods are bought for £1, if the stall costs £20 a day to run, if only £40-worth of stock can be afforded at any one time, at what price should sales be made?"

"If sold at £2 per item, "overheads" are covered after 20 sales, total costs after 30, and whatever the sales price after that it is all surplus. The market can be played accordingly. The lowest average price for which all 40 items can be sold without making a loss is £1.50. If only 30 can be sold an average price of £2.50 is needed to make an acceptable profit". And so on.

These relationships are governed by measuring where the "breakeven" points lie, which can be done by simple calculation once the information is organised properly. Buying or manufacturing policies—what? at what price? in what quantity?—can then be laid down with confidence. The specific nature of the product is unimportant. Its price/cost/demand relationship is.

Conversely, the record is strewn with Product-strong companies, on the face of it having magnificent commercial potential, who in practice perform indifferently or even go under because the equivalent commercial instinct is not present in the same strength. Indeed it can often become submerged and lost sight of altogether by that very technical excellence on which the company has built its reputation. Some of the most pre-eminent names spring to mind, from Rolls-Royce downwards. In contrast the Barrow Boy can afford to go to the West Indies on holiday every year.

If you, as Managing Director, are not complete master of such factors in your own company then the enclosed schedules are designed to help. The issues are by no means commonsense. For instance, in the attached example the January Actuals show a company making a loss that has a stronger, better cash flow than one making a profit, with a greater chance of living within its overdraft limits—a seemingly absurd contention. Likewise it seems illogical that uncertainties or errors in stock valuations cannot affect the overall cash flow pattern and can therefore safely be ignored.

It needs a certain amount of painstaking work to come to grips with the principles involved and to really master such issues, but it is hoped that the detailed explanations given in the following pages will help you to do so and do so successfully. The purpose is not so much to achieve good profitability for your company but to provide a stable and secure financial base from which it can expand strongly and successfully. Such a business plan should be drawn up for the next 12 months and agreed with the Fund. Ideally, you should do all the work yourself in the first instance and only seek the help of your financial experts in putting the final seal of approval to the figures.

Should Fund investment get under way, the resulting format will form the blueprint for monitoring actual progress against Budget—January Actuals have been inserted in the attached example. In February, February's Actuals will replace the January Budget column, giving comparison with February Budget and so on. The comparison shows not just *whether* the cash flow is going wrong but *where* and *why* (e.g. debtors) so specific remedial action can be taken, and taken well ahead of any resultant cash flow crisis.

One particular simplification should be noted. All stocks, work in progress and finished goods are recorded by reference to their labour and materials content *only*. *No* overheads or mark-ups of any kind are included. This considerably simplifies the task of compiling the forecast and also allows the company to record only materials and labour costs on all stock and job cost records. The Fund legal agreements lay down that Actual progress is to be reported against Estimate within 14 days of the end of each month. To enable you to meet this deadline the introduction of such simplified records will be necessary, if not in use already. Again this is an area where your professional advisers will be able to help. The ultimate aim is to give you fingertip control and understanding of your company for a minimum of time, cost and effort as events unfold.

Good Luck.

B. C. J. Warnes, MA FCA.,

PROCEDURE FOR DRAWING-UP FORECASTS

The line references refer to the examples given on page 177.

I Estimate **Monthly Sales** at line (1), pre VAT, allowing for fact that:
   1) For start-ups, build-up is nearly always much slower and takes longer than expected, and starts later.
   2) Holiday months (e.g. July/August, December) are usually poor.
   3) Seasonality should properly be taken into account (e.g. peak sales pre-Christmas, poor January etc.)

II Deduct **Direct Sales Costs** (2) namely:
   1) Trade discounts,
   2) Any other discounts or commissions *calculated as a percentage of sales price,*
   3) Outward delivery costs, freight, duty etc.

III Decide on pricing policy e.g. percentage mark-up on labour and material costs to arrive at sales price. Express the resulting labour, material and direct sales-cost (Stage II above) as a percentage of sales price. The balance will be the Gross Margin percentage. Most companies need to achieve at least 30% Gross Margin to survive and really need between 40% and 70% to do well.

Insert **Gross Margin Percentage** at (23) and apply to Sales at (1) to give **Gross Margin** (12) by value, allowing for:
   1) for start-ups, additional costs incurred to complete design and development work and to produce, test, finalise and production-engineer any prototypes,
   2) problems likely to be encountered in early months of production until procedures are got right (resulting in extra material wastage, excessive labour hours etc.),

3) Defective work e.g. rejected product returned by the customer,
4) Pilferage of materials,
5) Supplier problems—late deliveries, wrong specification, additional costs from last minute buying etc.

All of which may result, particularly for start-ups, in low and possibly even negative margins for a period until the various problems can be identified and got right.

IV Estimate **Material Deliveries** (5) (including sub-contract parts) needed to build-up stocks to maintain uninterrupted production.

V Estimate the **Labour Costs** (6) needed to support production, allowing for the addition that needs to be made to basic wages for:
1) Employers' NHI, Pension Contributions etc.
2) Holiday pay entitlement.

VI Insert **Opening Stock** (4) for month 1, from the "Opening Balance" figures at (32) + (33) + (34).

VII Derive **Closing Stock** (10) for month 1 by summing lines (1) to (12). Insert as opening stock (4) for month 2. Repeat through to month 12.

Check the above stock figures are approximately correct as follows (material and labour content only):

Raw Material (32). If, say, 6 weeks production requirement is carried, January's Stock should total January's Material Purchases (5) plus half December's (5).

Work in Progress (33). If work takes, say, an average of one month to pass through the factory, January's Work in Progress should be equivalent to January's Cost of Sales (11).

Finished Goods (34). If, say, 2 months stock is carried, January's Finished Goods should be broadly equivalent to December's plus January's cost of sales (11).

Check **Closing Stock** (10)=(32)+(33)+(34) for the same month.

Check **Opening Stock** (4)=(32)+(33)+(34) for the previous month.

Note 1: If the above *very approximate* calculations show the opening and closing stocks previously inserted at (4) and (10) are seriously understated, monthly material purchases (Stage IV) and Labour costs (V) should be increased and the stock figures (VII) reworked.

Note 2: Stocks of packing materials, publicity leaflets, etc. should be included with Finished Goods (34). Any amounts actually *used* in the month in sales at (1) should be included in cost of sales (11).

Note 3: The following complexity is *not* recommended and for forecasting purposes should, if possible be ignored, but if the company insists on showing an "overhead" content in stocks, rather than valuing stocks at just labour and material cost, the content should be separated out of (33) and (34) and the total shown at (19), with (20) being the equivalent for the previous month.

VIII Estimate **Overheads** (marketing, administration, legal, accountancy, office, travel, etc.) and insert at (13). Allow for:

(1) Additional legal, etc. costs at start of new business,

(2) Any building renovation, removal, machinery installation, etc.

(3) During year, such factors as inflation of pay and staff increases.

Note: Ignore Interest (16) for the time being (see later).

IX Estimate the finance needed to support credit given to customers. If, say, two months credit is given, **Trade Debtors** (30) will be the total of last two months sales, so January Debtors will total January's sales (1) plus December's sales (1). Include any element of debtors financed by factors, i.e. show the *gross* amount owing to the company including what is owing to the factors. Assume **Other Debtors** (31) are zero for forecasting purposes.

X **Progress Payments** (35) can also be ignored for forecasting purposes. (These are amounts invoiced to the customer, whether or not yet paid for by him, before a contract is technically "completed", and down payments or advances before the contract starts, or progress payments during it. Note that such amounts should *not* be regarded as "sales" at (1) until the contract has been "*completed*", whereupon the *whole* contract value should be treated as a sale, regardless of when various parts were invoiced and when the work was actually done, all part payments to date also being removed from (35).)

XI **Trade Creditors** (37). If suppliers give, say, 2 months credit, January's trade creditors will be December's material deliveries (5) + January's material deliveries (5).

XII **Other Creditors** (38). Include PAYE, VAT, Interest owing and accrued expenses, etc. Assume, say, equivalent to current month's overheads (17), or ignore for forecasting purposes.

XIII Derive **Net Current Assets** (40) by deducting (39) from (36). (This figure should approximately equal total sales for the past three months, for a typical manufacturing company. If it does not, go back to stage VII.)

XIV Moving now on to the Cash Flow as such, derive the **Increase** or **(Decrease)** in **Net Current Assets** (41). January's (41) will be January's (40) less December's (40).

XV Estimate gross **Capital Expenditure** (42) in the month, for purchase of buildings, plant, vehicles, etc. (*before* deducting e.g. any Hire Purchase arrangements).

XVI **Research and Development Expenditure.** Ignore (43) for forecasting purposes. Any labour and material cost included in (5) and (6), which has been diverted to Research and Development in the month, should be taken out again at (7). Include under administrative costs (13) total labour and material costs together with all direct salary costs etc. related to R & D. Deduct at (21) total R & D capitalised in month and insert at (43).

XVII Derive (44) = (41) + (42) + (43), giving the gross additional funding need in the month.

Insert at (45) **Pre-tax Profits (Losses)** from (22) and "add back" at (46) and (47) respectively any **depreciation** or **amortisation** included in (13), to arrive at **Cash Profits (Losses)** (48).

XVIII Cash Profits (48) will of course *reduce* the monthly net cash requirement and so need to be *deducted* from (44). Cash Losses (45) on the other hand will of course *increase* it and need to be *added*.

Profits are also reduced by interest charges (16) calculated on total borrowings (57), which in turn depend on profits. To break this vicious circle assume, initially, that interest (16) is zero. Derive a rough profit (loss) figure for month 1 and *deduct*, if a *profit*, from (44) to arrive at the rough **net cash requirement** (49). *Add* if a *loss*.

XIX Insert **Opening Balances** prior to the start of the 12 month period at (50) to (56) and total (57). Add to this the rough cash requirement at (49) for month 1 to arrive at a new total borrowing figure (57) as at the end of month 1.

XX Calculate **Interest,** for one month, on the rough total (57) and insert at (16) for month 1. Derive (17), (18) and (22). Insert the more accurate figure at (45) and rework **Total Borrowings** (57) at the end of month 1. Derive **Closing Overdraft** (56) for month 1, having inserted the relevant closing balances for **Factoring** (54), **Loans** (51), (52), and **Hire Purchase** (53).

XXI Work through the same cycle for month 2. And so on to month 12, which will then show peak funding need and what month it occurs.

XXII Calculate **Breakeven Point** (24) i.e. the level of turnover needed just to cover overheads (17), at the gross margin percentage in question (23) i.e. (17)×100÷(23).

At 25% gross margin every £4K* of sales above breakeven will produce a profit of £1K, every £4K below breakeven a loss of £1K. The company can be controlled accordingly by comparing *order intake* (25) and *orders in hand* (27) with *actual sales* (1).

Note that if the Gross Margin the company *thinks* it is going to achieve (26) and (28), as worked out from its Costing and Pricing data, begins to be substantially higher than is *actually* being achieved (23), the Costing and Pricing assumptions should immediately be rechecked to bring the two into line. The accuracy of the gross margin percentage calculated at (23) in turn should be frequently checked, particularly in the early months of a new company, by basing closing stock (10) on *physical stocktakes* (labour and materials only) until broad agreement begins to emerge. The task is often a tedious one for a period, but any company that does not know its *real* gross margins is likely to get into undue trouble, possibly very quickly.

MONTHLY MONITORING

Within 14 days of the end of each month, at least approximate results for the month should be inserted (January Actual in the example) for comparison with Budget. Next month, February's Actuals will over-write January's Budget to give comparison with February Budget. And so on.

*£K=£'000.   £4K=£4,000, etc.

Immediate rebudgeting for the rest of the year should take place whenever it becomes apparent from the emerging pattern of Actuals that the assumptions on which the Budget has been compiled are inaccurate, in order to give accurate warning as far as possible into the future of impending problems.

Useful additions that can be made to the layout are:
- (a) To insert Actual and Budget Year-To-Date columns to the left of the Monthly Profit and Loss Account.
- (b) To split the Cost of Sales section into two, showing materials (in opening stock, plus purchases less in closing stock), to arrive at a sub-total Value Added, and then deducting labour (in opening stock plus direct payroll less in closing stock), to arrive, as before, at Gross Margin.
- (c) To insert the monthly balance sheets. Lines (40) and (50) to (57) already give most of the balances. Fixed Assets are of course updated from (42) and (46); ditto intangibles (43) and (47); ditto retained profits (45).
- (d) To show, under all the columns, Creditor Strain, Net Creditor Strain and 'days' for Debtors, Stock and Creditors (Chapter VIII).
- (e) To maintain, say, four to six Actual columns to the left and nine to seven Budget columns (respectively) to the right. Each month, another month's budget is added and the earliest month's actual dropped; the other eight to six months' budget columns (i.e. apart from the current month being compared with actual) are updated in the light of the latest month's results, thereby projecting forward an accurate overdraft forecast.

MONTHLY PROFIT H FLOW (£'000)

	Actual				Budget									
Ref		D	J	J	F	A	M	J	J	A	S	O	N	D
						per Balance Sheet								
(1)	**Total Sales**	3·0	5·0	10·0	10·0	24·0	26·0	28·0	22·0	20·0	27·0	35·0	40·0	23·0
(2)	Direct Sales Costs	0·3	1·0	1·0	1·0	—	—	—	—	—	—	—	—	—
(3)	**Net Sales**	2·7	4·0	9·0	9·0									
						32·6	32·7	32·8	31·0	26·8	28·8	35·3	37·8	38·1
	Materials and Labour													
(4)	Opening Stock	22·0	25·0	25·0	27·0									
(5)	Material Deliveries	—	7·0	3·0	5·0									
(6)	Labour	5·0	4·0	5·0	3·0	56·6	58·7	60·8	53·0	46·8	55·8	70·3	77·8	61·1
(7)	(R & D)	—	—	—	—									
(10)	Closing Stock	(25·0)	(32·5)	(27·0)	(29·0)	12·0	11·0	10·0	5·0	—	7·0	17·0	20·0	10·0
(11)	**Cost of Sales**	2·0	3·5	6·0	6·0									
						12·0	11·0	10·0	5·0	—	7·0	17·0	20·0	10·0
(12)	**Gross Margin**	0·7	0·5	3·0	3·0									
						44·6	47·7	50·8	48·0	46·8	48·8	53·3	57·8	51·1
(13)	Administrative Costs	3·0	2·0	1·5	1·5									
(16)	Interest	0·6	0·5	0·6	0·6	in Month								Totals
						2·8	3·1	3·1	(2·8)	(1·2)	2·0	4·5	4·5	(6·7)	11·1
(17)	**Total Overheads**	3·6	2·5	2·1	2·1	—	—	—	—	—	6·0	—	—	—	21·0
(18)	**Net**	(2·9)	(2·0)	0·9	0·9									
(19)	Overheads in Closing Stock	—	—	—	—	2·8	3·1	3·1	(2·8)	(1·2)	8·0	4·5	4·5	(6·7)	32·1
(20)	(*Less* in Opening Stock)	—	—	—	—									
(21)	(Sundry Income, etc.)	—	—	—	—	0·6	1·2	1·2	(3·6)	0·6	1·0	6·5	2·5	(6·5)	6·6
						0·4	0·4	0·4	0·4	0·4	0·4	0·4	0·4	0·4	4·5
(22)	**Pre Tax Profit (Loss)**	(2·9)	(2·0)	0·9	0·9									
(23)	**Gross Margin Percentage**					1·0	1·6	1·6	(3·2)	1·0	1·4	6·9	2·9	(6·1)	11·1
	(12) × 100 ÷ (1)	23·3	10·0	30·0	30·0									
						1·8	1·5	1·5	0·4	(2·2)	6·6	(2·4)	1·6	(0·6)	21·0
(24)	**Breakeven Point**													
	(17) × 100 ÷ (23)	15·4	25·0	7·0	7·0	nces per Balance Sheet								
(25)	**Orders Taken in Month**		1·0	10·0		14·5	14·5	14·5	14·0	14·0	14·0	13·5	13·5	13·5
(26)	Estimated GM%	40·0	26·0			7·9	7·8	7·7	7·6	7·5	7·4	7·3	7·2	7·1
(27)	**Orders In Hand at Month end**	11·0	16·0			38·0	39·6	41·2	42·2	40·1	46·8	45·0	46·7	46·2
(28)	Estimated GM%	27·0	27·0			60·4	61·9	63·4	63·8	61·6	68·2	65·8	67·4	66·8